UNTOUCHABLE CHICAGO

A Ride Through Prohibition

By Don Fielding

a/k/a Al Dente

Edited by Grace Kuikman

Untouchable Times & Tours
Chicago, Illinois
www.gangstertour.com
ISBN: 978-0-615-31426-6

Table of Contents

Acknowledgements

I would like to thank my wife, Cindy, for her constant inspiration; my partner "Southside" Craig Alton for his patience and encouragement; our Untouchable Tours gangster guides "Shoulders" Randy Craig, Wayne "Big Julie" Juhlin, and Lon "Louie" Withers for their many years in our "gang," and for taking up the slack on the street during the past year when I've been immersed in this Untouchable Tour of my own; and my dear friends Grace Kuikman, Susan Johnston and Joanna Rybus for their invaluable technical assistance.

Don Fielding

Introduction

I remember dropping over to Don Fielding's house just over 20 years ago, finding him in the middle of a pile of books, immersed in the history of Chicago's gangsters and the Prohibition Era.

Don was doing research for the first Untouchable Tour, a new venture with his wife Cindy Fielding, a talented artist and top notch business woman, and his brother-in-law Craig Alton who had cut his "performance" teeth on WBEZ radio. These three creative talents collaborated on a ride through Prohibition Era Chicago that was entertaining (all the guides are in gangster costume and in character) as well as historically accurate. Cindy, Don and Craig knew they were creating a product for an eager public. Even though Al Capone arrived in Chicago in 1919 and was sent to Alcatraz for tax evasion by 1934, visitors to Chicago remain fascinated by Big Al and the Windy City's larger-than-life stories of the Roaring Twenties.

When Don (then known as Dixie Don) and Craig, a/k/a Southside first hit the streets, they gave the tour in the car. Response was immediate and positive. Within a few months, the fledgling company had purchased an old school bus, had it painted black, sprayed with fake bullet holes, decorated with a shooting gallery of gangster photos, and trademarked with the message: UNTOUCHABLE TOURS, Chicago's Original Gangster Tour.

Though the buses are bigger, better, and certainly more climate-controlled, they are still instantly recognizable as they roll through the streets where Al Capone, Bugs Moran, Dion O'Banion and Diamond Jim Colosimo ran their vice operations more than 80 years ago. As the tour's popularity grew, the company hired actors as guides, outfitting their "outfit"with spats, fedoras, pin striped suits and gangster identities. Suddenly guys with names like Shoulders, Big Jake, Dutch and Knuckles were tourists' favorite new pals in Chicago sightseeing.

Every year 40,000 visitors take a ride the hot spots and hit spots of Prohibiton era Chicago on the Untouchable Tour. They hail from around the world -- as far away as Europe, Japan, Australia, South America and Russia. The unique and, well, untouchable tour has been profiled in dozens of international newspapers and magazines, and featured on radio, television, the internet, and in the movies.

As famous for its facts as it is for its fun, Untouchable Tours recently celebrated its 20th anniversary, and Don finally stayed off the streets long enough to document his amazing knowledge about Prohibition Era Chicago in this book. And it's all right here: the north siders and south siders, dirty cops, windy politicians, first families of vice, bootleggers, ladies in red, and lots more. Enjoy the ride!

Grace Kuikman

Chapter 1

What Made the 1920s Roar? Prohibition

Chicago got the well-deserved reputation for big-time gangsters back in the Roaring Twenties. What gave the boys a jumpstart on all the action was the United States government. Giving in to pressure from the Women's Christian Temperance Union and a host of other misguided do-gooders, the politicians in Washington, D.C. ratified the 18th Amendment to the Constitution, effective on January 17, 1920. This law, which was in effect until December 5, 1933 (almost fourteen years), made it a federal crime to manufacture, sell or

William Hale "Big Bill" Thompson is sworn in as Chicago's Mayor.

transport alcoholic beverages. No beer? No wine? No booze? No way!

Since these libations were legally prohibited, this law became known as Prohibition. Some guys said, "Hey, we'll drink to that. Now we can make big money as bootleggers." "Bootleggers" is an old term that originated down South in the "bible-belt" where it had long been locally illegal to sell alcohol. The moonshiners would go around with sample bottles of moonshine whisky tucked into the tops of their boots.

A survey of Chicago residents revealed that, six-to-one, the local population was against this law. They could scarcely believe that the government would seriously attempt to enforce such an infringement upon personal habits. The citizenry had no intention of voluntarily complying with such a ludicrous ordinance.

The Mayor of Chicago, **William Hale "Big Bill" Thompson** declared himself completely opposed to the law and personally "wetter than the middle of the Atlantic Ocean." As a matter of fact, following his reelection in 1928, he hosted a raucous celebration that attracted so many revelers that the boat used as the "party-barge" sank due to overloading its capacity. His Honor was photographed trudging through the knee-deep muck of Belmont Harbor with his whisky-bottle held safely aloft.

There was no doubt that the Mayor was going to do nothing to encourage his police force to enforce a law so alien to his constituency and so antithetical to his own personal tastes. He pointed out that this law was not only unreasonable and unfair, it was un-American. That viewpoint had been furthered long before by no less an authority than the 16th President of the United States, Abraham Lincoln. The Great Emancipator from Illinois had said in 1860, when the temperance movement began, "Laws of prohibition go against everything that the government of this country stands for." Why, it would be downright unpatriotic to willingly comply with a law that denied personal freedom!

It is significant that the national census of 1920 indicated that among Chicago's first generation foreign-born immigrant population there was a cultural tradition of social drinking. Twenty seven percent of the new arrivals were from Germany, the country that practically claims to having invented beer. Twenty four percent of the recent immigrants were hard-working Polish laborers who relished a glass of beer after slaving long hours at the Union Stockyards. Twelve percent had arrived from Ireland, where sharing a pint along with a good story was the national pastime. It was unthinkable to the five percent immigrant society of Italians that they could be expected to wash down the Sunday family dinner without even a glass of homemade wine.

Legally it was possible to enjoy a mug of homebrewed beer or a glass of local cellar-vintage wine. The Volstead Act of Prohibition (named after the Senator from Minnesota who sponsored the bill that authorized its funding) contained a provision that granted some slight relief from its constraints. A loophole in the law allowed the domestic production of not more than one hundred gallons of beer and fifty gallons of wine per household per year. The sale of these beverages was still unlawful. Distilled spirits were prohibited entirely. Select wineries could manufacture limited amounts of wine for sale to churches for sacramental purposes.

Whisky "for medicinal purposes only" was distilled by licensed distilleries in Kentucky. This amber-colored "medicine" was available at local pharmacies to patients for whom physicians had supplied the necessary prescription. This window of opportunity was quickly seized upon by enterprising opportunists who trafficked in forged scripts, as well as by some unscrupulous druggists who would dilute their stock with adulterants (sometimes even deadly wood alcohol) to stretch their inventory.

The shipments of whisky were often hijacked *en route* to the government warehouses where they were stored prior to delivery to the local apothecaries. The warehouses themselves were frequently robbed at gunpoint by ambitious, sophisticated criminal organizations. Fortunately, most of the medicinal whisky did make it to the local drugstore. It was sorely needed by the growing patient population suffering under the strain of a range of maladies for which this amber elixir seemed the proper cure.

Set against this background was an informal criminal underworld that had existed in

Chicago since its inception in 1833, as a boisterous brawling commercial hub on the edge of the frontier. The very term "underworld" is thought to have been coined locally to describe the horrid dens of depravity that operated within a vast network of subterranean caverns below the city's surface during the 1800s.

With the enactment of Prohibition, the floodgates of opportunity were opened wide for men with ambition and moxie who previously had little or no chance of becoming wealthy. They could now join the party. Pre-prohibition area taverns were transformed into speakeasies overnight. In Chicago these clandestine bars numbered in the hundreds. Eventually, every one of these watering holes came under the "protection" of one of the neighborhood gangs that would invariably become affiliated with one of the powerful, prominent criminal organizations.

Speakeasies ran the gamut from fancy, "members only" establishments to the corner taverns to the more numerous "blind pigs", which numbered in the thousands. Blind pigs were run by independent, small time entrepreneurs, who would set up shop in garages, basements or apartments. These enterprises were dependent upon their owners having a contact through which they could acquire beer and booze without arousing the ire of the real operators.

Dion O'Banion

Chapter 2

The Beer Wars

Having established the origins and obvious financial incentives for involvement in the trade of alcoholic beverages, we can move forward with the story. During the Prohibition era, the "beer wars" gave Chicago the reputation as something closely resembling a lawless town on the frontier of the old Wild West. Indeed, some of the characters in the story do, in fact, bring to mind some of the bushwackers, stagecoach robbers and gunslingers of an earlier time.

There was never a more colorful, daring, enigmatic, beloved or detested character in theses tales than Mister **Dean (or Dion or Deanie) O'Banion**. Following the death of his mother, this lad of thirteen years moved with his father from a small town in rural Illinois to the big city. His father was a plasterer who did the best that he could for the boy, but young Dion O'Banion was seldom supervised during his youthful days on the streets of an area aptly known as "Little Hell". Little Hell was an Irish and Italian slum on the near northwest side of Chicago encompassing the area recently known for the Cabrini Green housing projects. Here he learned how to fight, speak Italian and blend with the rowdies.

Young O'Banion was briefly a student at Holy Name Cathedral School. He was an altar boy and a welcome addition to the choir, being blessed with a beautiful Irish-tenor voice. Despite some deportment issues, the priests briefly considered that this young fellow might even have a calling to the vocation. Unknown to them was the fact that his interests tended strongly toward more secular directions. He and his young cohorts in a youthful gang called the Little Hellions devoted themselves to becoming accomplished jackrollers. They would jump drunks and bums in the alleys and steal their "jack" (money). The seminary did not seem to loom on O'Banion's horizon.

In his later teens Deanie graduated to the job of "slugger" for the Hearst Newspaper Syndicate. His job description was simple. He was to assure that Hearst Newspaper vendors had the advantage of the most lucrative sales locations. Trespassing competitors were to be slugged, beaten and battered to within an inch of their lives. He was good at what he did and rarely had to make repeat visits to the same corners.

Viola & Dion O'Bannion

Despite his combative temperament, Dion had a charismatic personality that quickly enabled him to gain the trust and friendship of the lads who took up with him in his adventures. His daring and moxie led him to expand into the field of burglary and safecracking. It was a short step from strong-arm robbery to hijacking liquor shipments when Prohibition became the law of the land. For the record, he hijacked a whole truckload of liquor by sucker-punching a truck driver with a right hook in front of a crowd of bystanders in the middle of downtown on the third day of Prohibition! On a whim, when he was delayed from an alleyway as a truck was slowly backing into traffic, Dion surmised correctly that the vehicle was transporting liquor. He dragged the driver out of the cab, deposited him upon the sidewalk, then slowly drove away with the goods, to the bewildered astonishment of the stunned onlookers.

But O'Banion had a soft, sentimental side to his personality, as well. He had a lifelong fascination with flowers, along with a natural talent for their aesthetic arrangement. This proved to be a profitable sideline when he bought into part-ownership of the Schofield Flower Shop at 612 North State Street. Its prime location, directly across from Holy Name Cathedral, made it the obvious florist for weddings and funerals, and at the center for classy Catholic functions.

O'Banion's other consuming passion was his lovely wife, Viola. They lived in the apartment above the shop. They were in each other's company constantly, except, of course, when he had to put on his other hat and see to business matters that she didn't need to know about. He took great pains to shield her from the coarse side of his personality.

Dion O'Banion used the Schofield Flower Shop as his "front" for gang operations.

Dion was a devoted churchgoer, perhaps because he had an overabundance of transgressions on his conscience. While he had no reluctance to pull a gun and plug someone, he did have strict limits to the conduct he allowed himself and others. His Catholic-conscience led him to hold strong feelings about prostitution and honesty. He wouldn't tolerate the former and insisted upon the latter. He must have played hooky the day that "Thou Shall Not Kill" was the lesson at Holy Name Cathedral School. Hey, nobody's perfect!

O'Banion was scrupulously honest with his customers in both his floral and alcohol businesses. He insisted upon high-quality goods only. This stance presented conflict with some of his less ethical rivals in the liquor trade, most notably the 'Terrible Gennas" of Taylor Street. Animosity also existed between O'Banion and the Torrio-Capone organization. The disagreement centered on their repeated overtures to O'Banion to promote the business of prostitution in his area. He had utter contempt for men who would profit this way at the expense of poor women. He held that this was an insult to the Holy Mother herself. When reporters queried him regarding this subject he responded loudly, "I ain't no pimp!"

There was never a more close-knit, loyal or dedicated gang in Chicago than the north side gang of the O'Banion outfit. They were a multi-ethnic crew composed of Irishmen, Italians, Poles and Jews. Despite being hampered by a noticeable limp (the result of a fall as a boy when he unsuccessfully attempted to hitch a free ride on a streetcar), O'Banion was still physically imposing by virtue of his fearlessness, daring and quick fists. He was a natural-born leader and pleasantly disarming, despite his volatile temper. The poor "down-and-outer" could always count on O'Banion for a handout. If he found out about some poor crippled kid who needed an operation, he was always first in line to foot the bill and cover the expense.

The northsiders and the southsiders seemed, at the beginning of the era, capable of settling their differences in a businesslike manner. This uneasy truce was shattered after O'Banion engineered a joint venture with south side kingpin Johnny Torrio. The deal was to be that the two would operate the north side Siben Brewery and share its profits. This partnership was shattered when O'Banion arranged a police raid on the premises at a time during which he would personally be absent, but both Torrio and Capone would be present.

Mr. Torrio had a previous conviction for a Volstead Act violation. Now, as a twice-convicted violator, he was sentenced to a month-long stint in the Cook County Jail. His attorneys forestalled the incarceration for several months. As luck would have it, Torrio suffered injuries which will be elaborated upon later in these chronicles; his delicate medical condition, along with the threat of bodily-injury, were sufficient persuasion to the judiciary to allow him to serve his sentence in the north shore Lake County jail in Waukegan, Illinois.

Needless to say, O'Banion's recklessness and deceit snuffed out any potential for the south side outfit as an ally in Dion's escalating conflict with the Genna brothers of Taylor Street. This family was known as the Terrible Gennas because they had long preyed upon their own people as Black Handers. They extorted money from their hapless fellow immigrants by threatening to doom them forever via the dreaded *Malocchio* (the Evil Eye). If the parties didn't respond to esoteric threats, they generally responded to shotgun pellets.

Prohibition was a liberating event for many people throughout Little Italy. The Terrible Gennas were the first gang to enter into the wholesale moonshine industry. Their formerly victimized neighbors could now earn $15 a day staying close to home and running stills that produced alcohol for about $1 a gallon that sold for $6 a gallon. Since it was approximately 90 percent pure alcohol, it was necessary to cut it drastically before it was somewhat fit for human consumption. If you didn't want to dilute it, you could use it full strength as paint stripper. In order to give their clear liquor the appearance of whiskey, they added coal tar, creosote or prune juice, resulting in a brownish, java-like hue. For flavor, they added maple syrup.

The Genna Clan

Chapter 3

Upping the Stakes: Rotgut and Murder

The Genna clan of six brothers was bossed by **"Bloody" Angelo Genna.** He was the youngest, but the most treacherous of the family. Angelo had no apparent reluctance to have his adversaries murdered. This Sicilian family reveled in their status as the rulers of their little corner of the world. They derived a great deal of pleasure in the ostentatious display of their wealth. Annually, the Genna family promenaded to their front row seats at the Opera, then housed at the Auditorium Theatre on Michigan Avenue. Afterward, they would adjourn next door to the Gold Room of the Congress Hotel for an opulent meal.

Angelo had a running disagreement with the O'Banion gang because of Dion's adamant refusal to add the Gennas' rotgut to his inventory. This animosity came to a head on November 11, 1924. Ironically, the date set forth to commemorate the end of The Great War (the "war to end all wars") marked the beginning of an acceleration in warfare among Chicago's competing underworld players. Whatever truces previously in place would shortly be shattered. Emboldened by his ascension to the throne of power within the Sicilian community as the elected President of the *Unione Sicilana*, the time was ripe for Angelo Genna to engineer the hit on Dion O'Banion.

The occasion for this momentous assassination was the day of the funeral of the most recent President of the Sicilian Union, the highly regarded **Mike Merlo.** Merlo had died of natural causes following a tenure during which he had gained the admiration of not only his own people, but the community at-large, for his efforts to better the lot of Italian immigrants. The Schofield Flower Shop was doing a brisk business filling orders for the elaborate funeral service scheduled for later in the day. At age twenty-six, Angela Genna now assumed the post of President.

Frankie Yale

According to Mr. William Crutchfield, a porter for the Schofield Flower Shop, he overheard Mr. O'Banion greet some gentlemen with, "Hello boys, are you here for the flowers for Merlo's funeral?" Following this salutation, six shots were fired. O'Banion lay in a pool of blood as assailants fled. With a fleeting-glimpse of the escaping killers, Crutchfield could only describe them as short, dark and "Eyetalian" looking. The most educated guess is that the three hitmen were **Frankie Yale** (Francesco Uale) from New York, along with the gunsels **John (Giovanni) Scalise** and **Alberto Anselmi.**

Frankie Yale was briefly detained for questioning by the Chicago police when he attempted to board a train bound for New York City several hours after the shooting. He had a ready-made, plausible alibi for his whereabouts at the time of the crime. Scalise and Anselmi had only recently arrived from Sicily. Their anonymity shielded them from suspicion. But they would not avoid notoriety forever. Their misadventures had only just begun.

The reins of the north side gang fell unto the capable hands of **Earl "Little Hymie" Weiss**. He was short, powerfully built and terrifying. He was aggressive in temperament and apparently fearless. Despite the repeated protests of **Johnny Torrio** and his young protégé, **Al Capone,** regarding their innocence, Hymie Weiss was utterly convinced that they were accomplices in the murder of his beloved friend Dion O'Banion. Weiss assumed that Torrio and Capone had sought revenge for the Sieben Brewery incident. His resolute intentions were never in doubt. He told the duo that, "The only business that I'll have with you two is when I'm standing over your dead bodies with a pistol."

True to his word, Mr. Weiss, along with **George "Bugs" Moran**, set about the task of eliminating the south side leadership. For an overture to this symphony of gunshots, there was a pitched gun battle during the Christmas season of 1924. Weiss stood on the running board of a sedan while exchanging shots with Al Capone and **Frankie Rio** as they exited a court building. Spectators who viewed this prolonged firefight must have thought that they were viewing the filming of a cowboy movie.

Frankie Rio

Johnny "The Fox" Torrio

Chapter 4

North Side, South Side – There's War All Around the Town

The new year was ushered in by a much more professional plot, set to take place in January of 1925. **Johnny Torrio** had been so successful in the capacity of head of the south side criminal enterprise that he began to let his guard down. He had become so lax regarding issues of personal security that he seemed to regard himself as a legit businessman. In truth, he had always been in the field of commercialized vice (gambling, bootlegging and prostitution) as strictly a business. If people wanted to pay for such pleasures, then why shouldn't those who took the initiative in providing them make a profit by doing so? Torrio personally abhorred violence, only advocating its application as a last resort. He personally never fired a shot or carried a gun, but he knew plenty of other guys who did!

The northsiders put a "tail" on Johnny, discreetly shadowing his every movement. They discovered that Torrio frequently gave his bodyguards leave to go home early. He would then take the train home unaccompanied, enjoying the daily newspaper as his fellow-commuters were unaware that this light-built, dapper businessman was the kingpin of organized crime in Chicago in the mid-point of the Roaring Twenties. Neither he nor they could possibly anticipate that he would shortly be a news item in the daily "birdcage liner".

On the afternoon of January 24, 1925, Mr. Torrio had sent the boys home early in anticipation of an impending snowstorm, so that they could be with their families. Things had been so routine within the south side mob lately, the atmosphere had become practically mellow, except, of course, for the occasional necessity of arson, beating and the murder of rivals and reticent saloonkeepers. Once home, Johnny Torrio and his wife Margaret rarely went out except for a night of dinner and theater or the occasional shopping spree. They preferred quiet evenings together, amusing themselves with board games and pleasant conversations, generally retiring early for a good night's sleep. Mr. Torrio would rise early to a hearty breakfast that would energize him to "hit the bricks" and resume his daily routine. This bucolic existence was due to change forever.

The swiftly falling snow muffled Johnny's footsteps as he approached his residence at 7011 South Clyde Avenue on the city's south side. This calm was fractured when, as he was walking up his front steps, he heard a shout of, "Hey, Johnny!" followed by three shotgun blasts. One load of buckshot punctured his gut, a second peppered his chest, while a third caught the side of his neck as he spun around in response to hearing his name called. Little doubt exists that the assailants were none other than **Hymie Weiss** and his second-in-command, **George "Bugs" Moran**. A kid observed one of the men (Weiss?) dash over to the prone-figure of Torrio with an automatic pistol only to have it click in misfire as he attempted to deliver a fatal shot to the head. As bystanders quickly began to gather, the gunmen jumped into a waiting sedan and made a fast getaway assuming, no doubt, that their target was being left for dead!

An ambulance was summoned. Mr. Torrio was rushed to a hospital where his injuries were found to not be life-threatening. He was treated and given a private room for convalescence. A squad of ready and able men was assigned by Johnny's lieutenant, **Alphonse Capone,** to stand around-the-clock at Torrio's bedside and throughout the hospital corridors to thwart any attempt to finish him off.

Capone (who called the eighteen years older Torrio, "Papa Johnny" out of respect for his fatherly guidance) proclaimed loudly, "Whoever did this, I'll put 'em on the spot!" Papa Johnny, ever the diplomat, counseled retreat rather than revenge. The "godfather" of modern day organized crime was through with Chicago. He told young Capone, "Al, it's all yours. All that I want out of Chicago is out alive."

Mr. Torrio returned to Brooklyn, New York. Only once more did he return to Chicago. That visit was during Al Capone's 1931 trial for tax evasion. Much to the chagrin of Capone, Torrio sat quietly in the back of the courtroom as a spectator, averting his eyes whenever Al attempted to make eye contact, eschewing Capone's efforts to make personal approaches.

Torrio became a *consigliare* (trusted advisor) to Charles "Lucky" Luciano, Meyer Lansky, and Benjamin "Bugsy" Siegel in their gambling operations in Havana, Cuba and later on in Las Vegas. He died peacefully in his barber's chair in Brooklyn in 1958 at the age of 75.

Al Capone

So, in 1925, the twenty-six-year old Alphonse Capone inherited the position of ruler of Chicago's underworld, at least in the south side portion, which encompassed the Union Stockyards, vast factory areas, and territory extending all the way to the steel mills of East Chicago and Gary, Indiana. Despite peaceful entreaties, "Little Hymie" Weiss persisted in his efforts to eliminate Capone. The most flamboyant attack occurred on the morning of September 20, 1926, when Al and his bodyguard, **Frankie Rio**, were enjoying a leisurely breakfast in the cafe of the Hawthorne Hotel in Cicero, Al's suburban stronghold just outside Chicago's city limits.

As they sipped steamy coffee from mugs, they heard what sounded like gunfire from the next block. Capone rushed to the window to see what was going down. Frankie rushed over and told Al, "Get down, Boss! It's a setup!" No sooner had he said this than a caravan of sedans paraded by slowly with their occupants firing Thompson submachine guns in all directions. Hundreds of slugs shattered the windows and walls of the Hawthorne Hotel, though miraculously failing to even wound any of occupants. As Al, Frankie and a dozen customers were frozen to the floor, Weiss himself brazenly stood in the middle of Twenty Second Street blazing away with a Tommy gun blasting bullets into the building until he leaped into the back of a getaway car.

The only person injured was an innocent bystander. A tourist couple from Louisiana was sitting in their automobile in front of the Hawthorne Hotel, hoping to get a glimpse of Al Capone or some other famous Chicago gangster so they would have a story to tell the folks back home. They definitely got a story to recount and much more than they had bargained for. A ricochet bullet hit their windshield and a sliver of glass lodged in the lady's eye. A doctor at a nearby hospital easily removed it, leaving no permanent damage. When he was made aware of the mishap, Al paid for the medical expenses and personally gave the lady ten thousand dollars in compensation for her inconvenience. True or untrue, it's a nice story!

Capone was not so generous with Earl "Little Hymie" Weiss. On October 11, 1926, the north side boss was gunned down by hit men who had camped out on the second floor of an apartment building at the southwest corner of State and Superior streets. They had been there for about a week, according to their landlady who said that they rarely left the apartment except to procure takeaway food from a local greasy spoon restaurant. Their rent had been paid a month in advance and they had left the place littered with cigar stubs and cigarette butts. Evidently, the primary attraction for the renters had been the excellent line-of-fire between their window and the front of Holy Name Cathedral.

Weiss still used the Schofield flower shop as his front, although he was not florally inclined. As he and his companions were crossing the street from their fancy touring car, parked at the front of the church, they were greeted by a barrage of machine gun fire from at least two gunmen. Hymie caught thirty five slugs. His driver was killed. His lawyer and a local politician were wounded but survived. This quartet had been returning from the Criminal Courts building on Hubbard Street. A judge had just granted Weiss a continuance on a bootlegging charge. He would miss his scheduled court date due to a death in his immediate family. His twenty four-year-old wife Josephine was left to mourn the loss of her husband. Hopefully, she was somewhat consoled by the one million dollars cash rumored to be stashed in their home. George "Bugs" Moran took over the north side crew but, more about him later on.

Big Al Capone

Chapter 5

The Early Years of Al Capone

Just who was this fellow, Al Capone? He was born on January 12, 1899 in Brooklyn, New York to Gabrielle and Theresa Capone. His parents had immigrated to the United States from Naples, Italy in 1895. From Ellis Island they joined the large Italian immigrant community in Brooklyn, settling in the Five Points neighborhood on Garfield Avenue.

Mrs. Capone gave birth to seven sons who were followed by two daughters, Matilda and Muriel. Alphonse was the middle son. Mr. Capone worked as a barber. Mrs. Capone did piecework sewing jobs at home.

Al, a likeable, big kid, was an average student and left school after the sixth grade. Poor kids from one of the toughest sections of Brooklyn were more interested in making money than acquiring book learning. His first foray into the field of private enterprise was as the proprietor of a shoeshine stand at the age of thirteen. He was proud and happy to have his own little business that enabled a bit of independence as well as a means of "chipping in" to help the family financially. Sadly, this was all shattered by an older, jealous cousin who knocked the stand over and trashed it. Upon discovering the identity of the culprit, Al caught the kid alone and beat him to a pulp. He then vowed that nobody would ever again dare to rip him off and expect to get away with it without suffering dire consequences. He was true to his word.

The major opportunities in his neighborhood seemed to be in the field of criminal activity. A pal of his was a rough neck Sicilian immigrant named Charlie "Lucky" Luciano. The two became members of a local gang whose main rivals were the Irish boys competing with them for the waterfront area adjoining the Brooklyn Navy Yard. Control of that area, with its saloons and dives catering to sailors, led to "easy-money" opportunities. Capone's considerable physical strength earned him a regular job as a bouncer at a local dive called the Harvard Inn. It was owned by a fellow named Frankie Yale. The joke, obviously, was that the Anglicized pronunciation of his Italian name was "Yale-E". This character reappears at various points in the saga of Al Capone.

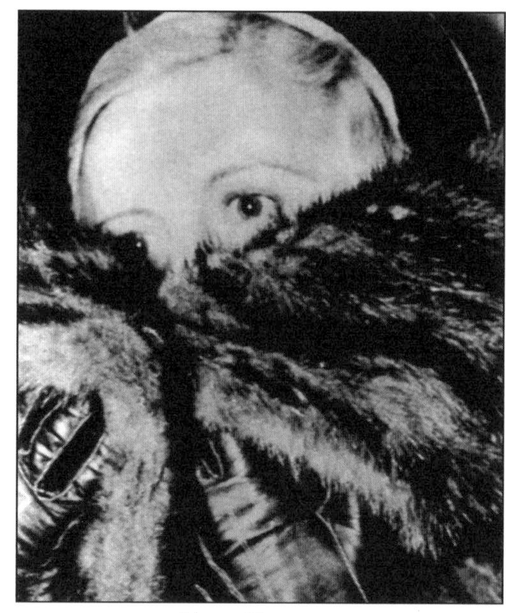

Mae Capone

An unfortunate incident occurred at this joint in 1918 that would forever give the world an impression of Al Capone. One evening Al, at that moment a perhaps intoxicated nineteen-year-old, became sufficiently emboldened to approach a young lady seated at a table with several of her friends. He whispered an off color compliment into her ear. She immediately blushed a vivid shade of crimson in embarrassment. Her brother, Franco Galluccio, asked what was the remark that made her so upset. Upon hearing that the drunken comment was, "Baby, you've got a beautiful ass!" he leaped across the table with a stiletto knife.

Gallucci's reponse to Capone's ill-advised romantic overture was, "you can't talk that way to my sister!" He then went for Capone's throat, slashing viciously four times. Al staggered backwards sufficiently to avoid his death, but suffered deep incisions from earlobe to jaw line leaving scars that would forever give a somewhat sinister appearance to his otherwise somewhat jolly countenance. Capone swore revenge, but he and Gallucci were brought before the local capo (boss) and ordered to bury the hatchet (but not into each other).

Capone carefully powdered his cheek to camouflage the disfigurement that earned him the detested moniker "Scarface". Years later, as a celebrity of sorts, he generally only allowed himself to be photographed from his "good side"; his left cheek was generally hidden from view.

Al preferred to be called Mr. Capone, the Big Fella, Big Al or Snorkey. He was particularly

The Four Deuces

pleased to be called the latter since it was 1920s slang for a classy, elegant dresser. He may have had his faults, but nobody ever accused him of being ill-tailored.

Fortune smiled upon Al in the person of a lovely Irish-American lass named **Mary Coughlin.** She was generally known as Mae. Her close friends called her Josephine. She brought forward Al's more tender instincts. They married and she gave birth to their son in 1920. He was christened Albert Francis, but was generally known as "Sonny". Al doted on his son and in later years they enjoyed attending baseball games together.

Capone and his young pregnant wife had made a hasty exit from New York in 1919. Allegedly, the "big fella" got into a dispute with an Irish gang member. Foregoing a lot of verbal sparring, Al let his fists do the talking. They spoke all too loudly, leaving the other lad nearly dead. Fearing retribution (not to mention a possible murder charge), Al made contact through intermediaries with Mr. John Torrio (formerly of Brooklyn) and was offered employment in Chicago. In late December, the Capones arrived at Union Station on Canal Street. There was no brass band or even a stranger to greet them. Mae was shivering from the cold. Al didn't even have an overcoat to lend her. He had thirty eight cents in one pocket and a thirty eight caliber pistol in the other. This was a less than auspicious beginning to a career that would assume legendary proportions.

The streetcar took the Capones to the south side office of Torrio. He arranged their lodging nearby and introduced Al to the Boss, "Big Jim" Colosimo. Al's initial assignment was at the Four Deuces, a joint located at 2222 South Wabash Avenue. This notorious establishment raked in the dough. Al's job was to rope guys from the street in to the first floor saloon with the offer of the coldest beer in town. There were "games of chance" on the second floor. If the patron had any money, there was an open invitation to make the acquaintance of the "nice girls" who were housed on the third and forth floors.

In the event that any of these gentlemen should become too rowdy, Capone's job description required that he also give them the "bum's rush" by introducing them to the alleyway exit underneath the elevated train tracks. This on-the-job training would serve him well in years hence, when he became the leading figure in Chicago's hospitality industry.

"Diamond Jim" Colosimo

Chapter 6

Diamond Jim & Johnny 'The Fox'

The "Deuces" was in the heart of what had long been called the "Levee District" due to its proximity to the Chicago River. Riverboat gamblers and their female consorts along with an assortment of pimps, prostitutes and hustlers had made their way to Chicago during the Civil War to service the Union Army quartered locally. Down South the riverbanks are frequently buttressed by mounded earthenworks called levees. Thus came the nickname for the area that was plied by these new arrivals, many who were from New Orleans. Their imported expertise ultimately made the Levee District the most infamous area of its kind in the entire western world.

The kingpin of the Levee District at the time of Al's arrival in 1919, was a colorful, gregarious fellow by the name of **Jim Colosimo.** He had arrived in Chicago several decades earlier as a teenage immigrant from Naples by way of Brooklyn. Like most immigrants to this day, Colosimo's initial employment was as a laborer. He started out as a section hand on the railroad, most likely as a waterboy for the thirsty workmen. His next promotion of sorts would have been to the better paying role of a "gandydancer". That was the title of the men assigned the job of working as a team to carry the heavy iron rails. The men would position the rails between their legs and do a sort of stutter step movement

The Levee District

in coordination. As a footnote, the rails were manufactured by the Gandy Manufacturing Company of Chicago, thus the origin of the term "gandydancer".

Jim was a bright boy who quickly discovered that there were less labor-intensive ways of making a living in Chicago. He caught on as a street sweeper with the city Department of Streets and Sanitation. He found that the obvious path to promotion was based upon "clout" (influence) with the local ward heelers who doled out jobs to their constituents as political patronage. He ingratiated himself to the "Lords of the Levee", Messrs. **John "Bathhouse" Coughlin** (no relation to Mrs. Capone) and **Michael "Hinky Dink" Kenna.** Colosimo gained merit in their eyes by organizing his fellow street sweepers into a voting bloc sworn in allegiance to the Kenna-Coughlin 1st Ward organization.

Colosimo was a handsome man with an engaging personality. Always on the prowl for enhanced opportunity, he surveyed the landscape and determined that his future would be brighter in the private sector. The transplanted New England establishment controlled the real wealth, the Irish had a stronghold on the police and fire departments, while the Germans and Scandinavians controlled the construction trades. For certain, Jim didn't want to join the Poles and Slavs standing knee-deep in stinky slime, wrestling animal carcasses in the Union Stockyards. He fancied himself as a Romeo, better equipped for dancing in the hedonistic underworld of Chicago than laboring in the depressing, boring, spirit-ruining tasks to which so many immigrants (and natives alike) found themselves relegated.

Jim's fortune was made when he caught the eye of a successful madam of a house of ill-repute who was charmed by his advances. Herself an immigrant from Sicily, she was named **Victoria Moresco.** Years older than Colosimo, not attractive by any standard of beauty, but sufficiently wealthy to arouse his ardor, he soon proposed marriage. The combination of her business savvy and his personal charm and political connections enabled them to build a chain of brothels that produced a fortune. In commemoration of their first wedding anniversary, Jim presented his bride with the surprise gift of a fancy new bordello, named "The Victoria" in her honor. What woman wouldn't be flattered by such a sentimental tribute?

Their enterprise was lucrative enough to allow Colosimo to indulge his obsession as a collector of diamonds. His enthusiasm for acquiring these sparkling gems became a real fetish. He wore diamond rings on every finger of both hands; had diamond-studded cufflinks; sported a diamond encrusted belt buckle; blinded onlookers with his four karat tie clasp; held his socks up with diamond covered sock garters; and passed the time while conducting business by thoughtlessly playing with loose diamonds if he grew bored by the discussion. He became known, for obvious reasons, as "Diamond Jim" Colosimo.

Jim's fixation on pure crystallized carbon didn't hamper his business interests. The brothels sold a commodity that was in continuous demand. Victoria was a skillful manager of their finances and overseer of other retail business interests. "Diamond Jim" had the resources to expand their holdings into a more respectable area. What could be more natural for an Italian than to open a restaurant specializing in food fit for the Caesars and Cleopatras of Chicago?

Colosimo was a brilliant impresario. He was skilled at "glad-handing" the local politicians and society "swells" as well as moving with ease among the denizens of the underworld. He played the role of gracious host to the hilt at Colosimo's Café. This opulent nightspot located at 2126 South Wabash Avenue, in the heart of the tenderloin, was lavishly appointed. The chandeliers were gold-plated, the wallpaper was green velvet, the wine list was impressive, and the food preparation impeccable. A unique feature was the hydraulic dance floor with a full orchestra that would arise majestically from the basement, suddenly appearing to the astounded guests as though by magic. For as little as two bits (25 cents), customers in 1919 could get bread, salad, pasta and a glass of wine followed by a swell floorshow. As a bonus, they might even get a peek at the likes of famous figures, including Charlie Chaplin, Al Jolsen, Sophie Tucker, or Jim's boyhood friend from Naples, opera star Enrico Caruso.

Colosimo's rise to the top had not been without difficult, dangerous challenges. A

Colosimo's Restaurant.

few years earlier there had been extortion attempts by *La Mano Nera*, Italian for "The Black Hand". This was a freelance criminal enterprise with ancient origins back in the old country. Preying upon their own people (sometimes even their own family members), these scoundrels would muscle in on their fellow immigrants who had achieved a measure of success in their adopted country and might be susceptible to their strong-arm tactics. Typically, members of The Black Hand would slip a syrupy-sweet note under a door that would read something like the following (in Italian, of course):

Dear, Kind, Gracious and Esteemed Sir,

It is an honor for us to be in a position to offer congratulations to you in recognition of your wonderful success in your recent business affairs. We wish to share in your good fortune to the tune of one thousand dollars cash delivered to us in a brown paper sack at a time and place of our choosing. We will appreciate your kind gift to us. If you do not comply with our humble request, we will blow up your home at a time when the entire family is present and asleep. We look forward to your cheerful, positive response.

This sinister epistle would then be signed with a handprint blotted in black ink. Failure to respond could result in more dire threats or the promised actions.

The Colosimos had initially remitted payments to The Black Hand, counting them as just an expected cost of doing business. Eventually, as they made the payments without a whimper, the extortion demands became too costly. Victoria was advised by her brother to contact a second cousin in Brooklyn who had gained a reputation there as a criminal mastermind. At the request of the Colosimos (along with the reality that he was currently "hot" in New York), young Johnny "The Fox" Torrio came to their aid in 1912.

Johnny never fired a pistol or carried a weapon. He was not a physically imposing man, standing about five feet, nine inches tall and weighing one hundred fifty pounds. He personally abhorred violence and didn't advocate the "rough stuff" except as a last resort. He did have various acquaintances however, who could supply "muscle" whenever, wherever and however necessary.

Dispensing of the troublesome "Black Handers" was a simple matter for Torrio. He arranged a rendezvous beneath the Archer Avenue-Clark Street underpass to deliver their payoff. Following a cordial exchange, Torrio merely walked away after handing off the bag of money. For fear of appearing rude, he turned back to wave goodbye, but they didn't wave back. They were in no position to acknowledge his courtesy. Their throats had been cut by some gentlemen who had been crouched nearby in the bushes all the while. Torrio shrugged his shoulders at their sudden disappearance. He then walked home, enjoying the peacefully calm summer evening. There were no more attempts by La Mano Nera to contact the Colosimos.

Johnny Torrio matured into a formidable figure. Colosimo gradually became a celebrity who enjoyed basking in his status and wealth while leaving the details of his business interests to his second-in-command. The brothels, gambling joints and saloons had blossomed into a small empire by the time Al Capone arrived in Chicago. Meanwhile, Mrs. Victoria Moresco Colosimo was being neglected, cast aside and taken for granted as Diamond Jim played around with her money. Hell hath no such wrath as a woman scorned!

Diamond Jim with Dale, the second Mrs. Colosimo.

Chapter 7

The End of Diamond Jim

During the first few months of Prohibition, Al was making the hefty sum of twenty-five bucks a week. While this clearly was not "big money", it was about the average amount of the expected payday for a working man at the time. Ambition soon stirred within the young man. Mrs. Capone had just delivered their baby boy. Al felt both pride and an increased sense of responsibility. Despite his faults, not the least of which were his occasional adulterous visits to the upper floors of the Four Deuces, Al was a devoted family man who took his responsibilities deadly seriously.

Prohibition quickly became an exercise in frustration for Johnny Torrio and Al Capone. Various individuals were beginning to carve out and make their fortunes quickly. By hook or crook, alcohol supplies were being obtained. Taverns were converted into speakeasies. Relationships were entered among gang members, as well as between their leadership and the local constabulary. The police were always on the lookout for a means to supplement their meager pay. Payola to them and the local politicians was a budgeted expense for the bootleggers.

Meanwhile, Torrio and Capone could only look upon this action and lick their chops at the prospect of entering the fray. Their ambitions were being thwarted at every turn. O'Banion was dead set against any expansion of their prostitution activities into his territory. Compounding the situation was Colosimo's refusal to enter into the wholesale beer and liquor trade. His response to their repeated requests was, "Forget about it, fellas.

Colosimo was gunned down in his own restaurant.

Things are going along swell as it is. Anyway, that's a federal rap that even I can't fix with the boys downtown."

That response was definitely not the one that Torrio and Capone were looking for. The boys could barely conceal their disappointment as this stalemate lingered, not that Colosimo noticed. The problem was that he had developed a case of the "middle-age crazies" that was clouding his better judgment. At age forty five, Colosimo's flirtations with Miss Dale Winter, a lovely young lady less than half his age who was a singer in his cabaret, morphed into a full blown fling. Their affair precipitated a divorce from Victoria followed by a lavish wedding to his young bride. As the couple set about their honeymoon, they left a trail of disgruntled people in their wake.

Johnny and Al thought that Colosimo had gone *pazzo* (crazy) by letting the fabulous business opportunity of bootlegging slip through their fingers. Victoria Colosimo nee Moresco bitterly commented, "I raised a boy into a man, and what do I have to show for it for all those years?" Her two "made" Mafia brothers were openly upset at this major interruption to their cash flow. It is a very bad idea to incur the wrath of a Sicilian woman and her Mafioso kin.

The month of May did not turn out to be the least bit merry for the newlyweds. On the spring morning of May 11, 1920, "Diamond Jim" had to cut short his usually casual breakfast with Dale to go to his restaurant early. He had a business meeting with Jim O'Leary, a prominent south side gambler who was the only child of Mrs. Katherine O'Leary of "the Great Chicago Fire" fame. Colosimo arranged himself in the front lobby, avoiding the hubbub and slippery floors of the club's interior as employees went about their daily chores in preparation for another evening of business. He waited (impatiently, no doubt, given his gregarious nature) for a meeting that wasn't to be.

The silence was interrupted by the sound of gunfire. A lone gunman had leaped from the telephone booth behind him, emptying four rounds from a .38 caliber revolver into the back of Colosimo's skull. A startled employee rushed from the kitchen only to discover the lifeless corpse of his boss. During the murder investigation this witness could only tell the detectives that he had but a fleeting glimpse of a short, dark, "Italian looking" man, running south down Wabash Avenue. The identity of the assassin could not be confirmed through identification by police mug shots. Those photographs are generally of frontal and side angles, rather than posterior views.

Everyone was left to wildly conjecture in the absence of any credible evidence. Some

Cook County Sheriff Hoffman exhibiting confiscated evidence.

thought that the gunman was Frankie Yale. He was a contract hitman from Brooklyn who fit the rough description of the only witness. Additionally, he was an acquaintance of both Torrio and Capone, circumstantially thought to have a financial motive in Colosimo's demise. But, of course, though he had been in Chicago that day visiting friends, he was miles away at the time of the unfortunate incident.

Perhaps the brothers of the jilted Victoria exacted revenge in defense of family honor. Nobody knew who did the deed, but everyone knew who was now in charge. Jim Colosimo's death was John Torrio's good fortune. The funeral was a lavish affair befitting a head of state. Ministers, big wig politicians, society dilettantes, entertainers, and prominent businessmen climbed all over each other in lavishing praise upon the departed soul. This rogue who had been a convicted white slaver, a greedy glutton, and a pimp was lauded in glowing orations praising his acts of charity and benevolence. As the first shovel full of dirt rattled against the outside of the coffin, Torrio and Capone hastily exited the cemetery to set into motion their long delayed entry into the industry of beer and booze.

Under the astutely cunning management of Johnny "The Fox" Torrio, the south side contingent quickly began to form a smoothly running enterprise. Their sphere of influence would eventually encompass the greater south side area with its stockyards, packing houses, steel mills and factories that virtually dotted the landscape. Along with this vast market, Chicago played host to hordes of visitors eager for a night on the town to enjoy its well-advertised diversions. In summary, Chicago was a huge market for alcohol, gambling, burlesque and prostitution. Whoever could be first to establish a foothold in supplying theses pleasures would be in a position to gain riches beyond their wildest dreams. The challenge after that would be to hold that position as challengers surfaced.

Some people just seem to have a flair for business. Johnny Torrio was definitely one of those people. He was professionally objective about his chosen occupation. Although he personally did not indulge in any of the vices that he marketed, he certainly did not begrudge others those pleasures. He was worldly enough to realize that men would be willing to pay for the "soft pleasures of life". The provision of these goods and services represented an entrepreneurial opportunity. His viewpoint was that commercialized vice was as legit a business as any other. Come to think of it, it was probably more honest than many other enterprises. He introduced professionalism into a field that had formerly been just rough-and-tumble, avoiding unnecessary violence in favor of negotiation.

Michael "Hinky Dink" Kenna (left) and John "Bathhouse" Coughlin

Chapter 8

The Politics of Profit

The first order of business was to develop a business plan that provided for staff development and expansion. Al Capone apprenticed at not only the Four Deuces, but also as manager of The Stateline Café in the southeastern suburb of Burnham. That town had an eighteen-year-old "Boy Mayor" installed in office by the mob. "The Boys" had carte blanche to do whatever they wanted in Burnham. The Stateline Café literally straddled the Illinois-Indiana line. It was a rowdy bar, catering to roughneck clientele from the nearby steel mills. This "shot-and-a-beer" joint with some husky harlots was raided from both sides of the border by coppers seeking payoffs in compensation for "police protection". When the cops from one state or the other would enter, the patrons would scurry to the sanctuary of the other side of their jurisdiction thus avoiding arrest. There is no record of the lawmen from both states ever staging a simultaneous raid!

Johnny Torrio realized that the key to a successful operation depended largely on the degree to which the local power brokers could be relied upon to run interference with the legal authorities. He had inherited from Colosimo the sponsorship of two of the most powerful, influential members of the Chicago City Council. **Michael "Hinky Dink" Kenna** and **John "Bathhouse" Coughlin** ruled the 1st Ward uncontested and had done so since the 1890s. This area encompassed Torrio's area, as well as downtown with its lucrative hotels, restaurants and saloons.

"Hinky Dink" had acquired his nickname as a scrawny little kid selling newspapers. He was a cute, feisty young hustler, skilled in the art of salesmanship even as a lad standing about four foot ten (a height above which he barely rose). He parlayed his business acumen years later into ownership of the Workingmen's Exchange. This saloon featured the longest bar east of the Mississippi River, thirty-ounce schooners of beer, and the best nickel lunch in town. His clientele alone furnished enough votes to sway virtually any civic elections.

Favorable voter turn out was assured by affording free lodging in the flophouse above the saloon to any drunkard, drifter or petty thief loafing about town in the last weeks prior to a big election. They were free to graze over the free lunch counter for sustenance. At the close of the evening they were treated to the beer that had overflowed the glasses and spilled into the suds trough beneath the bar. In repayment for Kenna's generosity, these gentlemen were expected to rouse themselves into a semblance of sobriety on election day. They were then given a list of local polling places along with a punch card and a palm card with names of the candidates they were to vote for. Upon exiting the polling places, their cards would be punched and initialed by one of his men. At the close of the day, they would return to the Workingmen's Exchange and redeem their cards to the tune of twenty-five cents per punch. Civic-minded individuals could make as much a five bucks in a day.

"Hinky Dink" Kenna's initiative in employing these idlers resulted in his enjoying unquestioned influence in City Council Chambers. He was a taciturn little man whose "yea" or "nay" was usually the final say in matters coming before this august body. His vote was the first cast in a roll call, everyone else merely followed suit if they ever hoped to be reelected.

His esteemed colleague, "Bathhouse" John Coughlin had earned his moniker as a teenaged masseur in the steam rooms of the old Palmer House Hotel. The hotel had catered to wealthy businessmen and merchants from whom Coughlin picked up tips for making bucks, eavesdropping on conversations as clients relaxed on the tables. He gleaned that the least risk and (in the long run) most money was to be made by sticking to the "small stuff", making your fortune by way of small pops that didn't attract attention by upsetting someone's applecart.

Coughlin played the role of buffoon to the hilt, but he was as stupid as a fox. As soon as he was able to finance his own bathhouse, he opened the first one and followed it with almost a dozen others. His bathing parlors catered to the numerous hard working folks who looked forward to a scrub down that would only set them back a few cents. A hot bath seemed like a real luxury to the masses of people housed in lodging that lacked

Chicago Police stayed busy during the Roaring Twenties.

running water and indoor plumbing. Such a man who could supply a basic amenity as that provided by "Bathhouse" John was widely regarded as a public benefactor. His political acumen lay largely with his innate ability to identify with the common folk, especially those who inhabited the lower rungs, such as the operators of the saloons and bawdy houses. He famously disarmed (or armed) his critics with public orations of his audacious poetry. Some of his notable works include "Ode To A Bathhouse", "She Sleeps By The Drainage Canal", and the philosophical gem, "Why Did They Build the Lovely Lake So Close To The Horrible Shore?". To his credit, it was later discovered that most of his poems were "ghost-written"!

Councilman "Hinky Dink" Kenna provided a special service to his constituents. He gave his commercial constituents a list of preferred suppliers from whom they were expected to purchase those material items needed to conduct their businesses. Failing to patronize the preferred vendors could result in visits from City inspectors, loss of business, or other "dire consequences." Councilman "Bathhouse" Coughlin could be of assistance in the avoidance of "dire consequences". His adjunct profession was as an insurance

Mayor William Hale "Big Bill" Thompson

agent specializing in the areas of fire, theft and personal injury. These disastrous events could generally be avoided by his policy holders. It was uncanny how often those who declined the offer of his issuances of insurance suffered catastrophic events.

Just as Jim Colosimo had done before him, Johnny Torrio forked over a bit of tribute to the Kenna-Coughlin combine in exchange for their "clout" in City Hall. He did so as a matter of course, in the understanding that it was a reasonable, anticipated cost of doing business. They had a public franchise to dispense favors from the government. In a sense, Torrio was a concessionaire granted a license for his business by the largesse of these fine, distinguished representatives of the body politic. Messrs. Kenna and Coughlin could, with absolute confidence, guarantee that there would be no interference by the office of the Mayor upon the business of the 1st Ward.

The truth of the matter was that **Mayor William Hale "Big Bill" Thompson** was little inclined to do much of anything other than feeding his huge ego, partying and feathering his own nest. He had been a spoiled rich kid, whose family had cleaned up in real estate deals during the early days of the city. His youth had been misspent with rowdy friends gambling, racing horses at breakneck speed through town during drunken sprees, chasing around with loose women, and generally playing the fool. These youthful pursuits continued to occupy his attention for his entire life. Adult behavior seldom dampened his preoccupation with things pleasurable.

A lifelong aversion to legitimate forms of work led him to enter politics. His port of entry was the city's 2nd Ward. This area on the southern border of the Kenna-Coughlin turf was seen as "the Black belt" of Chicago. The city was highly racially segregated, with most folks of African-American ancestry residing within this area between "the Loop" (the downtown area encircled or looped by the elevated train tracks) and the Hyde Park neighborhood farther south dominated by the University of Chicago.

"Big Bill" found natural allies among the "policy kings" of this area. These gentlemen were somewhat analogous to the caucasian "wise guys". The main difference, beyond complexion, was that they had an extra card up their sleeves. In addition to the usual portfolio of illicit activities, they operated a type of lottery based upon digits corresponding to the closing numbers of the stock markets. In exchange for his guarantee of no police crackdowns on their activities, they guaranteed his election as their representative in City Hall. It was the votes from the black people of the 2nd Ward that catapulted him to the

Mayoralty in 1915. He was able to occupy that office until 1923, when he was booted out the first time. He was reelected in 1927, only to be drummed out of office in 1931, having bankrupted the city. During Thompson's initial acceptance speech he told his supporters, "Boys, it's our turn at the pig-trough, so let's feed!"

Hinky Dink & Bathhouse

Thompson's reign as the ruling monarch was characterized by "bread and circuses". He developed a reputation for bizarre behavior. He was seen frequently driving his convertible around town while wearing his trademark ten-gallon hat. Having spent his boyhood summers horsing around at his family's dude ranch in Colorado, he fancied himself a cowboy (albeit an urban one). To inject some life into what he considered too often dull and tedious City Council meetings, Thompson once staged a sort of rodeo in Council Chambers. He made a grand entrance astride his horse, decked out in western garb; followed by wranglers herding cattle. Fortunately, a stampede did not ensue.

Upon his reelection in 1928, following upon the heels of a one-term reform administration, Thompson entertained over one hundred celebrants aboard a leaky boat anchored in Belmont Harbor. The vessel was so overloaded with revelers that it slowly sank under their weight. Undaunted, the partiers joined His Honor in wading ashore through the knee deep water, whisky bottle held cheerfully aloft, to resume the party on dry land!

The Mayor's popularity was bolstered by his very generous giveaway programs. In a bid to be known as "Big Bill the Builder", his tenure produced an unprecedented number of construction projects, including public buildings, bridges and roads. The only drawback to his ambitions was that the projects outstripped the financial resources necessary to fund them. At the conclusion of his term, the city was flat broke as a result of his financial irresponsibility. He should get high marks for creativity, though. When the City was unable to make payroll, he issued "Big Bills". This was "currency" printed by the City redeemable at Marshall Field & Company and other stores, backed by Thompson's personal guarantee. The program was short-lived.

Maxwell Street

Chapter 9

Building a Bootlegging Empire

Johnny Torrio proved to be a mastermind when it came to building a bootlegging empire. He methodically consolidated the local players into a loose confederation, with subsidiary organizations feeding into them. The basic structure would be modeled along the lines of a consortium, rather than a pyramid. Plenary sessions were held around the city to gain their agreement regarding territorial borders. Inevitably, follow up meetings became necessary as "misunderstandings" arose.

There was a wide assortment of players on the scene. The Maxwell Street area, with its vast number of Jewish and eastern-European immigrants, was overseen by Maxie Eisenberg. He was dubbed, "King of the Pushcart Peddlers", in recognition of his success in organizing them into a self-protective merchant association operating within an area shown on maps as "the Ghetto". Jews were generally relegated to living and working within this confined area.

Directly to the south of Maxwell Street was "the Patch". This was an area of mostly Irish stockyard workers, presided over by the amiable duo of Terrance Druggan and Frankie Lake. The "Back-of-the-Yards" territory was hotly contested by longtime rivals **"Polack Joe" Saltis** and **Edward "Spike" O'Donnell.** Complicating the picture was the powerful political-athletic club known as "Ragen's Colts". Led by **Frank Ragen** (who later became a Cook County Commissioner), this tight-knit community partied, voted and fought as one. Their motto was, "hit one of us; you hit all of us!" Their area was courted by the outside elements of organized crime, but it was never subdued.

Edward "Spike" O'Donnell

The near west side around Taylor Street housed the Italian immigrant community. This teeming slum had generally been ungovernable throughout its existence. It was usurped early on by the "Black Handers" who ruled the largely uneducated, unprotected population through a combination of real and imagined threats. There were rogues who regularly patrolled the area with shotguns. They would extort tribute from the helpless residents. Sometimes the poor, superstitious folk who had been tossed into this frightening urban stewpot fresh "off-the-boat" and only recently removed from the Sicilian countryside, could be separated from their meager savings by *malocchio*, the dreaded "evil-eye". So great was their fear of the "look that can kill", they would accede to the demands of these predators of their own nationality.

A measure of propriety was briefly established by a local gentleman named **"Diamond Joe" Esposito**. A restaurateur possessed of a congenial-manner and a benevolent attitude toward his fellow *paisani* (countrymen), he was a beacon of hope for his people. Tragically, he was gunned down in broad daylight by the Terrible Gennas. They were a ruthless clan who were never destined to "come into the fold" alongside the other gangs, owing chiefly to their despicable disregard for anyone outside their immediate family.

The vast west side area beyond "Little Italy" was serviced by the "Klondike" O'Donnell boys (no relation to the southside O'Donnells). They had a cordial relationship with Torrio, as long as their personal holdings were not in any way compromised. The north side was an entirely different matter from the rest of the city. The story of the conflict between the south and the north sides runs through this entire saga. The description of their epic struggles

Maxwell Street vendors and shoppers.

will be elaborated fully as this saga develops and unfolds.

Beyond the city limits of Chicago lay the town of Cicero. This town, along with its neighbors, Berwyn and Stickney, proved to be extremely amicable toward the overtures of Mr. Torrio's free-spending representatives.

An additional measure of respect (fear) was engendered following the "Battle of Cicero" in 1924, during which Al's brother, Frank Capone, was killed by police in a gun battle on an overheated Election Day. Despite reinforcements from the Chicago Police Department in an effort to aid the outmanned Cicero Police, the Torrio-Capone brand of electioneering swept their slate of candidates into office.

In flight from the reformers of the Mayor Michael Dever administration in Chicago, this would be the new home office of their organization until "Big Bill" could be reinstalled to his rightful position. So complete was their control of this municipality that several years later Al Capone felt free to bounce the Mayor of Cicero down the City Hall steps when the official stepped out of line.

The local electorate welcomed these outsiders with their ample supplies of beer and money. This primarily Slavic, Catholic town had a voracious thirst for beer and no particular aversion to gambling, but they were rigidly, religiously opposed to houses of prostitution. They insisted that this sinful, corrupting influence be relegated to the neighboring towns. In exchange for this gracious concession, the south side outfit of Torrio and Capone was given the keys to the city. This arrangement was honored by both parties through the years, affording sanctuary to "the boys" while supplying a consistent revenue stream to the community. It is a beautiful thing to behold when men of good will can unite in common cause for a greater good!

Johnny Torrio was the only individual with the requisite moxie, experience and intelligence to capably bring these disparate groups under one umbrella. He already had a sophisticated business model in place. Matters related to accounting were under the guidance of **Jake "Greasy Thumb" Guzik,** a Polish Jew who was a financial wizard. He came by the label "Greasy Thumb" as a teenaged waiter at his uncle's fried chicken restaurant. He had the annoying habit of carrying customers' plates with his thumb planted squarely in the middle of their food. In later years, when these were stacks of currency to be enumerated, it was said that he could count the bills so rapidly that it was as though he had greased thumbs.

Jake "Greasy Thumb" Guzik

Supervision of the daily activities of the "marketing representatives" was handled by the street-savvy Alphonse Capone. He kept the boys on task and dispatched them to deal with customers whenever necessary. His authority was never questioned by his subordinates, but he managed with intelligence and prudence rather than belligerence. His natural instincts about people served him well as he matured. He developed real leadership skills, finely honed by rapidly acquired practical experience on the front line.

Strategic planning was the primary task of Mr. Torrio. Envisioning the big picture and then formulating a methodology for bringing it into focus became his grand obsession. Never content to prosper within narrow constrictions of geography, he sought to broaden his sphere of influence by sharing his genius with the other leaders…for a price, of course.

To get the ball rolling, Johnny arranged a sort of summit meeting at the Congress Hotel on Michigan Avenue in the spring of 1924. To counter the growing internecine warfare, a treaty was proposed whereby all parties would agree to respect one another's territorial boundaries. Furthermore, it was suggested by Mr. Torrio that he coordinate the alliance and equitably divide the downtown area with its many hotels and speakeasies among the parties. In compensation for this valuable service, he proposed that he receive a cut from the enterprises represented therein. While all were present there were only modest, mumbled words of dissent at the proposition, but no general agreement. When the parties retreated to their lairs, they scoffed at the audacity of Torrio's idea and went about business as usual.

Trouble was brewing on several fronts. The south side outfit was seemingly intent on expanding their commercialized prostitution operation into the north side. O'Banion insisted that he would never allow them to impose that particular enterprise upon his area. He felt that it was an affront to the Holy Mother and the Catholic Church; no way would he be a party to such an abomination. Meanwhile, the Genna brothers of Taylor Street had such an oversupply of their moonshine that they were now constantly imploring O'Banion to add their product to his inventory. Deanie adamantly insisted that his reputation as a merchant dealing in only quality goods precluded him from peddling their loathsome, inferior swill. It would have been well within his character to have voiced his feelings just that bluntly.

The daring little Dion O'Banion was always eager to press his luck. This was never more evident than in May 1924. The interests of O'Banion and Johnny Torrio had seemingly coalesced sometime earlier. To assure themselves a steady supply of their most marketable commodity, they had gone into partnership, purchasing the Sieben Brewery (most likely from prominent braumeister Josef Stensen). This amicable relationship was shattered on May 18, 1924 when Torrio and Capone were arrested for violation of the Volstead Act of Prohibition. It seemed that O'Banion had sold his fifty-percent interest in the brewery to Torrio the week before for $500,000, feigning a desire to retire from the rackets and enjoy life at the flower shop with his wife Viola. It appeared more than coincidental to Torrio and Capone that they were busted within a few days of shelling out all that cash.

Al was out of jail within hours. He had no previous arrest record at that point in time. Mr. Torrio was confronted with a very different situation. He was obliged to spend several weeks in jail because of a prior conviction on the same charge. To rub salt into the wound, after fleecing his business partners O'Banion was going around town bragging about how he had "really put one over on those grease balls!" His practical joke was no laughing matter to those whom he offended.

A stony silence had descended over the Chicago underworld. Everyone was going about their business, profits were escalating and whatever conflicts were in play were at least temporarily put on hold. The reality of the situation was that some parties were biding their move. Someone had determined that the morning of November 11, 1924, would be an auspicious date to pull the hit on the feisty florist. How ironic that Armistice Day, the day set aside to celebrate the conclusion of the Great War to end all wars, would be the date chosen to mark the commencement of a new round of warfare.

The Schofield Flower Shop had been busy for days preparing elaborate floral arrangements for the funeral of the esteemed president of the *Unione Siciliana* (Sicilian Union). Mike Merlo had died of natural causes while presiding with distinction over the most prestigious Italian society of the time. O'Banion's busy morning was rudely interrupted by a hail of gunfire by unknown assailants who had entered his shop, ostensibly to pick up flowers. Their dirty deed done, they sped away in a waiting sedan, leaving Dion O'Banion's lifeless corpse in their wake.

Al Capone and his lawyer take a break at the court house.

The Schofield Flower Shop had its biggest day ever the following week. The occasion was the sendoff for Mr. Dion O'Banion himself. The funeral cortege extended for nearly two miles. The hearse was preceded by twenty four flower cars. Such a large turnout attested to both his personal popularity as well as his prestige. He had always been a soft-touch for "down-and-outers" as well as for any poor kid who needed medical attention. His sentimentality and generosity contributed mightily to his charisma and the legendary degree of loyalty that he inspired among his men.

Who were the assassins? Were they hired guns brought in from out of town by Johnny Torrio? Was this payback for his deceit in the Sieben Brewery bust? Could the hitmen have been two recent rivals, John Scalise and Albert Anselmi from Marsala, Sicily, enforcing the wishes of the scorned Genna family? The frequent visitor Frankie Yale of Brooklyn was briefly detained by police later that day while attempting to board a train for New York.

Earl "Hymie" Weiss

He was released after being interrogated. He insisted that he was just another tourist who had been in town visiting friends who could vouch for his whereabouts at the time of the murder. Torrio and Capone proclaimed their innocence, but Hymie Weiss voiced his conviction that they were responsible for the death of his beloved friend. He vowed that they would pay the ultimate price for their transgression.

"Big Al" Capone chats with a police detective.

Chapter 10

The Ascension of Al Capone

Although Johnny Torrio extended the olive branch to Weiss, his overture was rebuffed. Johnny sought a return to business as usual, but Weiss responded, "The only business I'll have with you two guys is when I'm standing over your dead bodies with a pistol!" True to his word, Weiss attempted several hits on Capone during the next few weeks. In one, he attempted to gun down Capone as he was exiting a building on Michigan Avenue. Al took chase on the running board of a speeding automobile, firing at Weiss's escaping vehicle.

Following the aborted attempts on the life of Capone, Weiss targeted Johnny Torrio as a change of pace. Whereas Al always had his guard up warily, Torrio had become a bit lax regarding personal security. He had imprudently fallen into the custom of occasionally dismissing his bodyguards so that he could anonymously take public transportation home to his domicile just like any other businessman. Rich folk sometimes find amusement in doing things that the rest of us find tedious and boring.

The evening of January 24, 1925, Johnny sent the boys home early in anticipation of an advancing snowstorm. He looked forward to a quiet evening at home with his wife Margaret, snuggling beside the fireside following a pleasant dinner. It was not to be. As he was walking up the front steps to his home, he was perforated by buckshot from three shotgun blasts! One got him in the gut! One got him in the side of his chest! One grazed his throat! Hymie Weiss rushed over to deliver the promised bullet to the skull but the pistol misfired, to his disappointment. As startled onlookers began to gather, Weiss and Bugs Moran left Torrio for dead. Fortunately for Torrio, an ambulance was hastily summoned and quickly transported him to a nearby hospital where he received treatment.

The next day he summoned his protégé Al Capone to his bedside and in royal fashion passed the scepter to him with, "Al, it's all yours. All I want out of Chicago is out alive!" Thus began the reign of the newly crowned "King of Chicago", twenty six year old Alphonse "Scarface" Capone.

Ralph "Bottles" Capone

Torrio retreated to the sanctuary of New York leaving Mr. Capone to dominate gangland Chicago with a flair that would come to epitomize every caricature the public imagination could hold of a crime boss. More than 100 years after his birth, his story continues to hold a fascination.

Al Capone was thrust into the harsh glare of the news photographers' flash bulbs at the age of twenty six. Surrounded by fearsome rivals, he was immediately faced with an alarming set of challenges. First and foremost was the need to establish his credentials as leader of those loyalists already closest to him. Jake Guzik could be trusted to handle the finances. Frankie Rio would be his shield from the threat of physical harm. **"Machine Gun" Jack McGurn** was more than ready, willing and able to engage enemies in mortal combat. Additionally, he had cultivated and would maintain a fiercely loyal inner-circle of "standup guys" who would never cross him.

Frank Nitti, "The Enforcer"

Al's older brother **Ralph Capone** was known as "Bottles". His role was distribution manager for the liquor business. Whenever the speakeasy operators spotted Ralph entering their establishments, they knew that they would be purchasing a quantity of bottles. Younger brother Frank was an early casualty of the Capone brothers. He was shot and killed during the "Battle of Cicero". This fatality hardened Al's determination to hold fast to the hard won territory that was now stained by the blood of his own family. Matt Capone was the brother that disappeared from Chicago prior to Al taking over from Johnny Torrio. He left Chicago without any criminal record whatsoever, went to Colorado and, under an assumed name, became a policeman. He ultimately became a county sheriff whose real identity didn't become known until after his death.

The general manager of the organization was a Sicilian, Francesco Nitto, hereafter referred to by his assumed name: **Frank Nitti.** He was known as "The Enforcer". Commands from the "Big Fella" were expedited by Frank. Everyone understood that his directives were backed by the full power of the boss. Years later Nitti would become more of a public figure than he was during the 20s, but even then he remained as shadowy a figure as possible.

Nitti was adept at altering his appearance to evade adversaries. Sometimes he sported a mustache and slicked-back hair; sometimes not. Often he would change from business attire to workingman's overalls in the office. He would then depart in an old truck, rather than in the fancy sedan in which he had arrived earlier. He relished the role of being "the-man-behind-the-curtain". This allowed him the freedom to enjoy a personal life with his wife, to whom he was devoted and always faithful. This alone set him apart from most of his peers. They tended to be serial adulterers wherever an opportunity cropped up.

"Machine Gun" Jack McGurn

In Capone's and Nitti's absence the gang leader was **Hymie Levine**. He was unknown outside the inner circle of the Capone mob. His anonymity made him especially effective in a supernumary role. His only brief public appearance was when he was indicted for murder. The charges were subsequently dropped for lack of evidence. He disappeared into the nether regions of the underworld shortly thereafter.

The most colorful, flamboyant and feared member of Capone's cast of characters was **"Machine Gun" Jack McGurn.** He was born in Licata, Sicily on February 15, 1905, as Vincenzo Gibaldi. The family immigrated to Brooklyn when he was a small child. His natural father was murdered by New York mobsters in a case of mistaken identity. His mother married a gentleman named Angelo DeMora. The family moved to Chicago to open a grocery store on Vernon Park Place in the Little Italy neighborhood. Out of respect for his stepfather, young Vincenzo adopted the family name of DeMora.

When he was eighteen years old an event occurred that would render him simultaneously shattered and hardened for life. Two young punks staged an armed robbery upon Mr. DeMora's store. They shot and killed the unarmed man in the commission of the robbery. What the police assumed was robbery was actually something else. Angelo had been selling sugar to some local bootleggers who became incensed when they discovered him selling to their rivals as well! Young Vincenzo rushed to the crime scene as soon as he heard of the tragedy. He told the police at the scene, "You don't have to worry yourselves about this case. I'm big enough to take care of it myself." True to his word, he handled the case as judge, jury and executioner. Once he found out who the killers were, he cornered them and asked, "Why did you kill my old man?" They pleaded for their miserable lives with, "Please, Jack, we didn't know that was your old man! We just thought he was an old nickel-and-dimer!"

Vincenzo responded to their undiplomatic remarks with slugs from a 45. To punctuate his reply he placed nickels in their cold, dead hands to show who was really small change. He repeated this tradition of "designer killing" a couple of dozen times during his career as Chicago's premier hitman.

Vincenzo was very athletic and sought to test his boxing skills as a professional prizefighter. The boxing racket at that time was promoted principally to Irishmen who like to gamble on the outcome of the bouts. The best way to gain a spot on the fightcard was to be Irish or pretend to be. Vincenzo Gibaldi took the ring name of "Battling" Jack McGurn. From 1919, through 1921, he was a professional pug. The general consensus was that he could throw a punch, but he had a tendency to fold under a flurry of punches from his opponent. He was thus labeled "an umbrella".

Seeing no hope of ever being a contender, Jack dropped out of the ring but retained the name. He was on a mission to whack as many of the Genna mob as he could, and he didn't want to bring the family name into the sort of notoriety that was sure to follow. Jack was welcomed into the northside Circus Gang, which was headed up by Claude "Screwy" Maddox. This outfit was sort of a minor league farm team of Capone's. It wasn't long before Jack McGurn got called up to the big club following his quick success in bumping off a half dozen or so Sicilian gang members. His stock rose immeasurably when he was designated by Frank Nitti to be the triggerman for the hit on Hymie Weiss. That event would earn him the prefix "Machine Gun." Prior to that day he had generally used a revolver pistol to do his job. Ironically, Jack would be given Taylor Street as his territory years later, when it fell under Capone control.

Jack and Al became good friends. They shared an appreciation of wine, women and song as well as an enjoyment of the game of golf. McGurn was an occasional golf partner of Bing Crosby when he was in town during his years as a crooner. Jack was sufficiently accomplished on the links to qualify for the Western Open championship one year. It was too bad that Jack had to make an exit in the middle of the round, leaving his clubs on the green as he fled from police who had a warrant for his arrest!

Capone had his headquarters at the Metropole Hotel on Michigan Avenue.

Chapter 11

Hideouts & Hangouts

Al Capone was an actual person who lived an extraordinary life rather than a mere iconic figure. Let's attempt to bring him into finer focus.

Al was a physically imposing man. Standing five-feet, ten-inches tall and weighing in at about two hundred sixty pounds, he was well proportioned in a husky way. His scarred left cheek gave him a slightly sinister appearance that was softened somewhat by his broad-lipped smile, brooding "puppy dog" eyes, and engaging personality. When necessary, Al's demeanor could turn on a dime. He was about the last person on earth that you would want to anger, but his legendary temper was reserved for special occasions far removed from the public eye.

The attribute most admired by his compatriots was his unflinching integrity. His handshake was sufficient to seal a deal. Woe to those who would fail to hold up their end of the bargain. Guaranteeing fairness and loyalty, he commanded the respect of those he led. His motto was, "Al for all and all for Al!" The enterprise was a team with Al as coach and everyone playing their designated positions.

Occasionally there were certain individuals who lacked team spirit. They were summarily cut from the squad. Despite all the hyperbole in later years, Capone's inner circle consisted of not more than fifty associates. Most were of Italian ancestry, due primarily to a natural bond among first and second generation immigrants who shared a common cultural heritage in which English may not have been their first language.

Al connected well with Jews, Irish, German, Polish, and Anglo-Saxon nationalities. He would gladly do business with anyone. He was as American as apple pie in this outlook. Proudly displayed on his oversized desk at his Lexington Hotel headquarters were statues of elephants that symbolized his admiration for the Republican Party. Behind his high backed desk chair hung portraits of his favorite Republicans: Abraham Lincoln, George Washington and William Hale Thompson.

The Metropole Hotel at 2300 South Michigan Avenue was Capone's primary headquarters early on in his Chicago "business dealings." When Mayor Dever supplanted Big Bill Thompson in 1924, it had become expedient for Al to hightail it from the city. During that time he worked in Cicero, where he had the run of the town without any competition from other operators. Five miles due west on Twenty Second Street from the Metropole lay the town of Cicero. It was an ideal location for Capone and Torrio's command center. From his Cicero headquarters in the Hawthorne Inn Hotel at 4800 West Twenty Second Street, Al could easily drop in to check on the action at The Ship, The Hawthorne Smoke Shop, or any of their other gambling joints and speakeasies around town. These gambling rooms more than made up for any revenue from prostitution that he lost due to the ban on that particular sort of activity in Cicero.

The Cicero police provided security for Al's operation, while the local village officials snuffed out any attempts by outside authorities to encroach upon their jurisdiction. The location also enhanced Capone's alliances with various west side bootleggers, especially the O'Donnells and the cagey Welshman **Murray "The Camel" Humphreys.** Some people thought that Humphreys acquired that nickname due to his fondness for camel hair topcoats, while others insisted that it was a play on his surname. The latter gains some credence in light of the fact that some of the boys referred to him as "the Hump".

En route between the south side of Chicago and the town of Cicero in the enclave known as "Little Italy". Mr. Capone made a point of at least attempting to maintain a cordial relationship with the Sicilian community in that area. Since he was of Neapolitan rather than Sicilian ancestry, Al was ineligible for entry into the innermost sanctums of that society. There was existent a tradition that was called "the Mafia." It was a confederation of criminal gangs that controlled the areas where large numbers of Italian immigrants resided. The Mafia preyed upon their own people, but they would attempt to "muscle in" on others when given the opportunity. Capone's principal interest in dealing with the Gennas was based upon his desire to have access to that family's vast alky stores.

The funeral of "Bloody" Angelo Genna

The Genna family had immigrated to America from Marsala, Sicily, around the turn of the twentieth century. They were part of the tremendous migration of Italians that occurred between 1900 and 1915. As a matter if fact, eighty percent of all the immigrants to the United States during that period were from Italy.

Mr. Capone was firmly established by now as the premier leader in his field in Chicago. He commanded a small army of soldiers who enforced his commands as he oversaw an empire that encompassed booze, gambling, prostitution, and organized labor. He ruled with an iron fist when necessary, but preferred diplomacy, if possible.

Even with Capone's patronage, if not an actual alliance, the Gennas were lined up in the crosshairs of the persistent Mr. Hymie Weiss who continued Dion's blood feud with them as well as with the southsiders. The open warfare with the Genna brothers reached its conclusion in the spring of 1925. Weiss figured that he should strike quickly before the Gennas themselves initiated the inevitable. The bond between the Sicilians and Capone was growing noticeably stronger. The Gennas had strengthened those ties in the hope that Capone could somehow shield them from Weiss's recurring attempts to move in on their territory, and killing them all if given even half of a chance. Not content to simply boycott their lousy booze, Weiss and Bugs Moran had recently made a big show of making daylight visits to the Genna's turf. They were even seen walking down Taylor Street like they owned the place. When warned by the cop on the beat that they were really pushing their luck by being the area, Moran replied, "I wish one of those wops would show himself. I'm nuts to blow off some greaseball's head."

On May 26, 1925, "Bloody" Angelo Genna was driving to the Lakeshore Drive apartment that he shared with his new bride. He never made it home for dinner. Four men in an automobile pulled us beside his car and blasted him with more than a dozen slugs, blowing him to kingdom come. The assailants remain unknown, of course, just like all the gangland murderers during Prohibition. Not one of the cases was ever successfully prosecuted.

On June 13, 1925, just eighteen days following the death of Angelo, the always ferocious, psychopathic **Mike "The Devil" Genna** went down for the count in a gun battle with Chicago policemen following a high speed chase. The pursuit had been initiated when Mike, in the company of ace hitmen **John Scalise** and **Albert Anselmi,** went speeding through the south side in the belief that the Weiss-Moran gang was hot on his tail. His paranoia (they were nowhere in the vicinity at the time) incited him to drive erratically enough to crash into a light pole at Fifty-Fifth Street and Western Avenue. Genna, Scalise and Anselmi attempted to hoof it out of there. Their efforts resulted in Mike contracting a case of lead poisoning when police returned gunfire after he took a couple of shots at them and missed. Scalise and Anselmi were soon found cowering in hiding in the dressing room of a nearby clothing store and arrested. Even though police asserted that they too had fired shots in the direction of the pursuing officers, they never went to court to face charges. The attorneys for the government were out-lawyered. The talents of these two goons didn't go to waste. Their services were immediately made available to Al Capone, who was always on the lookout for men of their particular aptitude.

The funeral of **"Bloody" Angelo Genna** was even more expensive and elaborate than that of Dion O'Banion. And the funeral of Mike "The Devil" Genna was even more of a grand spectacle than Angelo's. Fortunately for Mama Genna, she was spared any more sendoffs for her sons. Since they observed an obvious pattern developing for the Genna brothers in Chicago, the family wisely retired to Sicily to buy some olive trees and get into the salad oil business in the hope that the change of climate would be good for their health. Anyway, public enthusiasm for these lavish, gaudy gangster funerals had waned to the point that such affairs had become rather "ho-hum."

A smiling Al Capone leaves the court building.

Chapter 12

The South Rises

The only intractable situation for the Capone outfit was the impasse with the Weiss-Moran contingent on the north side. This simmering conflict was a disaster waiting to happen. The threat of attack from Hymie Weiss kept Capone constantly on edge. He wanted to think that if he ignored the north side they would eventually lose interest. Wishing that they would go away was not getting the job done. Weiss appeared to be obsessed with moving in the direction of a collision course. On September 11, 1926, the die was cast that would let slip the dogs of war!

Al had every reason to feel safe and secure in the middle of Cicero, Illinois that beautiful autumn morning. Capone and his bodyguard, Frankie Rio, were leisurely sipping mugs of steaming hot joe in the coffee shop of the Hawthorne Hotel. There were only a few other diners there at mid-morning, so the place was quiet enough to allow them to ease into the day's agenda slowly…or so they thought.

The serenity was disturbed by the sound of gunfire from what seemed to start a block

George "Bugs" Moran

away and getting ever closer. Capone's initial reaction was to leap to his feet and run to the front window to see what was happening. Frankie grabbed him by the shoulders and dragged him away shouting, "Get down, Boss! It's a setup!" He called that shot right for they had no sooner than taken a nose dive under the nearest table than the window where they had been standing was blown apart by a fusillade of bullets!

Al and Frankie Rio wisely stayed glued to the floor for several more minutes in anticipation of more fireworks to follow. This turned out to be a very wise decision. The gunfire was merely the first of what witnesses later said was a convoy of eight automobiles that sped down Cermak Road with Tommy guns blazing out the side windows as the gunners within sprayed the front of the Hawthorne Inn with hundreds of bullets! A lone gunman (probably "Bugs" Moran, who always favored brown attire but was said to have been in khaki clothing head-to-toe) leapt out of the last car and raked the front of the building with machine gun fire! He then jumped into the backseat as the car sped away from the scene, leaving the street shrouded in the lingering, sulfurous smell of gunpowder amidst a haze of smoke that stung the eyes like teargas.

The window of the hotel and the adjoining coffee shop were blown out completely. The occupants of the café slowly, cautiously rose while attempting to avoid the glassy debris. As Capone and Rio looked around they were relieved and astounded to see not one drop of blood. The only casualty was an innocent bystander. A lady and her husband, visiting from Louisiana, were sitting in their automobile out front of the hotel hoping to get a glimpse of the famous Al Capone to tell the folks back home. They got an eyeful when a ricochet bullet hit their windshield and the woman got a sliver of glass in her eye. Hearing her crying outside when the smoke started to clear, Al discovered what had happened. He had one of his boys immediately drive her and her husband to the nearest hospital where a doctor was able to remove the glass from her eye, with no permanent damage. Al gave the lady ten thousand dollars to compensate her for her suffering and inconvenience. A tidy sum in 1926!

Shocked and momentarily stunned by this bold full assault, Capone realized that the time had come to exterminate pesty Hymie Weiss. Since Al had been attacked right in the heart of his own territory, it seemed like poetic justice to ambush Weiss at his headquarters, except with a much different outcome than the ineffective attack on Capone in Cicero. The hit would have to be executed very cleverly to obtain the desired result.

Holy Name Cathedral

The northsiders were astonished that their massive firepower had been so spectacularly impotent. They now had two strikes against them in their efforts to rub out south side bosses. They had merely wounded Johnny Torrio in their initial effort to avenge O'Banion's murder. In the attempt on the life of Al Capone, they had only managed to wound a tourist. Now, Weiss and Moran were facing an 0-and-2 count. One more strike and they were out! There could be no doubt in their minds that Al's fastball was going to be smokin' down the middle some time soon. They just didn't know when it was coming.

The northsiders took a defensive posture for once, laying low while curtailing their usual activities as much as possible. Some business matters couldn't be avoided. Court dates fell within that category. The morning of November 11, 1926, featured that agenda item on Hymie's calendar. There was a little matter of a bootlegging charge to reply to at the Criminal Courts building on Hubbard Street, six blocks away from the flower shop headquarters that was still home plate for the northsiders. Court wouldn't be a big deal. It was just a formality that Weiss and his lawyer would appear to seek yet another continuance before the charge was dropped, as always!

Next door to the Schofield Flower Shop there was a rooming house. Frank Nitti had one of his men rent a room for $8 a week that had a perfect vantage point for ambushing Hymie Weiss when he would approach the entrance to the shop. Nitti and "Machine Gun" Jack McGurn moved into the room and went on a stake out, waiting for the right moment to bag their prey. Informants kept them aware of Hymie's movements, but they wanted a clear shot at him when there were no innocent bystanders to get caught in the crossfire.

Hymie's widow, Josephine Weiss

At four o'clock that afternoon, Weiss's Cadillac pulled to a stop in his customary parking place in front of Holy Name Cathedral. A second sedan eased in behind, and its occupants climbed out. Hymie Weiss and his bodyguard, "Paddy" Murray, began walking across the street toward the flower shop with driver Sam Pellar a few paces behind them. The trailing vehicle had been driven by Benjamin Jacobs, the investigator for William O'Brien, Weiss's lawyer. The duo of Jacobs and O'Brien were still on the church side of the street when Hymie and Paddy were nearing the sidewalk in front of the shop.

They never made it.

"Machine Gun" McGurn let loose with a volley of Thompson submachine gun fire that chopped them down before they made it to the curb. Paddy Murray caught eight slugs in the head and body that killed him immediately. Hymie, similarly injured, managed to stay alive for a couple of hours, without regaining consciousness. His personal effects included a .45 caliber pistol, a set of Rosary beads, and $5,000. These were his usual accessories. He would frequently have his gun in his right hand while working the Rosary with his left as he was preparing to shoot somebody.

McGurn injured but didn't manage to dispose of, Pellar, Jacobs or O'Brien. He and Frank Nitti beat it out of the rooming house by way of the back rear stairs that led to the alley. They ditched the Tommy gun and a shotgun on top of a neighbor's dog house, then leaped into a getaway car.

When the assailants vanished, they left only a pile of cigar stubs, cigarette butts, empty beer bottles and takeaway containers from a nearby chop suey joint as evidence. The landlady could provide only a sketchy description of the men who had paid a month's rent in advance and kept to themselves for the week that they had been there. The coppers were clueless, and Mrs. Josephine Weiss was a twenty-four-year-old widow with some additional closet space and a rumored million dollars in cash that her husband had stashed away.

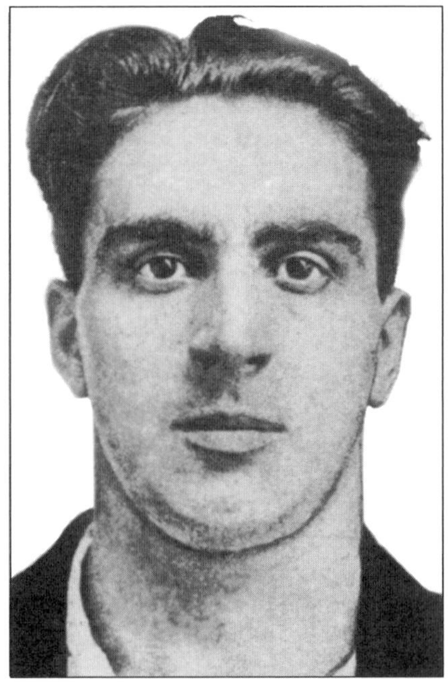
Vincent "The Schemer" Drucci

Suspicious fingers were pointed in the direction of Al Capone. He certainly had the means and motive to have Weiss rubbed out, but, "nobody could prove nuthin'". This hit ushered in an era during which the Bugs Moran-led north side gang remained a threat to the interest of the Capone empire, but the gang was not endowed with the degree of menace previously held. From time to time there would again be flare-ups however, the battles would not be as pitched or frequent as before. This vacuum allowed Capone relatively free reign over Chicago's underworld.

After the demise of "Little Hymie" Weiss, **Vincent "The Schemer" Drucci** briefly held the top spot on the north side totem pole. His tenure was abbreviated on April 4, 1927, when he wised off to some Chicago cops who were driving him to police headquarters for questioning. They said that he made a grab for a policeman's service revolver, which then accidentally discharged. This turn of events resulted in a detour to the morgue.

George "Bugs" Moran then took over the reins. Moran had always been wild and crazy. Newspaper reporters said that he was "buggy", meaning that he had "bugs in his head buzzing around" and should be in the "bughouse." His reputation for impetuous boldness was only enhanced when he tirelessly attempted to challenge Capone to do battle, "any time, any place, and any how." Moran was no dummy, but he was seemingly oblivious to the reality that his operation was decaying as rapidly as Al's was flourishing. Compared to Capone's operation, Moran's deal was strictly "small potatoes."

The sign on the truck says, "Capone! How much longer can he get away with it?"

Chapter 13

On a Winning Streak

Big Al really peaked in the year 1928. The dust on the Chicago battlefield had temporarily settled. Finally, the Capones could enjoy the fruits of their labors. Al had a modest but quite substantial home constructed for the family at 7244 South Prairie Avenue. The deed was in his mother's name. Being able to provide such a generous gift to his mama made Al's Italian heart proud! It was a quiet neighborhood of mostly German and Irish residents. As a matter of fact, the Capones were the only Italian family on the block. The home, a two flat, still stands in a well maintained area. Mama Therese and her daughter Matilda had a lovely apartment on the second floor. Al, Mae and Sonny were nestled on the first floor. There were several features that most homes in the area lacked, such as the cast iron burglar bars and a steel "jailhouse door" that were mortared into the basement bricks. There was no way that any intruders were going to barge in unexpectedly.

Home security should not have been a major worry. There was a Chicago Police Department squad car permanently parked in the street in front of the house. The rear of the home was amply guarded by some of Capone's men who were anchored along the garage and alleyway at all times. The Capone residence was probably the safest place in Chicago.

Later in 1928, the Capone's purchased a second home. They had rented a beautiful bayside mansion complete with a pool, tennis court and boat dock on Palm Island (across Biscayne Bay from Miami Beach) the previous winter. When it became available for purchase, Al jumped on the deal. He enjoyed being outdoors and loved fishing, as well as being able to lounge around the pool with family and friends.

The Capones were doing well and seemed to be under the illusion that their situation, while always tenuous, was somehow perfectly "normal." Perhaps if Al had been content to just cut out a piece of the action for himself and maintain a low profile, maybe things could have gone on indefinitely. That was not to be. Once you're in the mob there is no way to get out. You know too much and have accumulated too many enemies to be able to bow out gracefully.

All too often is the case that when guys get the big money, they also get the big head. Their head outgrows their hat and they start to believe that they are who the masses think they are. But when you start believing your own B.S., you are heading for a fall!

In the nine years since Prohibition began, Mr. Alphonse Capone (a/k/a Scarface, a/k/a Big Al, a/k/a The Big Fella, a/k/a Snorky) had become a celebrity on a grand scale. When he and "Machine Gun" Jack McGurn entered the stadium at Northwestern University for the 1928 football clash with Notre Dame, they were greeted by rousing cheers from the student body. The college kids felt a sort of kinship for these bootleggers who may have been the source of the "school spirit" within their game day hip flasks!

When the employees of Capone and Company enjoyed a day at the old ballpark to cheer on the White Sox or the Cubs, Al was afforded the courtesy of the ballplayers being quite willing to stop by his box seats to shake his hand and autograph a baseball for his son. There is a famous photograph of Al and Sonny with Cubs catcher Gabby Hartnett at Wrigley Field, with the entourage occupying the section all around them.

The most monumental public appearance of Mr. Capone during 1930 was when his image graced the cover of *Time Magazin*e. His mug plastered on the cover guaranteed increased circulation! Although he rarely allowed himself to be photographed from his scarred left side, he made an exception in this instance. Wearing his favorite Borsalino fedora while sporting a big Cheshire cat grin, his photograph appeared above the caption, "Scarface Al Capone, Chicago." At that moment in history, he symbolized Chicago for much of the world (to the dismay of the blue blood, silk-stocking crowd). The little guys, the "strap-hangers" on the streetcars and the average Joes enjoyed basking in his reflected glory as much as they enjoyed the libations provided by his breweries.

Big Al takes time off for a ball game.

We should take into consideration the reality that most people were not directly impacted by the sporadic outbreaks of internecine warfare among the competing factions of bootleggers and vice peddlers. To the huddled masses, Al Capone was a larger than life legend they would probably never lay eyes on in real life. They did somehow delight in that their geographical proximity to him somehow cast their humdrum lives in a different light. This gave them a hint of glory in the same way that sports fans vicariously revel in the antics of their heroes.

The vast fortune accumulated by Al Capone was the object of a great deal of speculation. One educated estimate of his personal gross income for the year of 1927 was $125 million. That figure represented the most income ever generated by a private individual in a single year in the history of the world until then! Even if that figure is way over inflated, it is still a whole lot of moolah. Mr. Capone was never accused of being stingy and miserly. His generosity was legendary. For instance, he opened a soup kitchen at 936 South State Street for poor fellas who were down on their luck. One of the grateful diners was seen and heard on a movie newsreel during the early thirties exclaiming, "If it weren't for Mr.

Al Capone, me and the boys woulda starved to death last winter!"

He arranged for deliveries of coal to poor families faced with the prospect of shivering through the bitter cold of a Chicago winter in their drafty, freezing flats. Christmas gifts for the children of Saint Columbanus parish, where his mother attended mass daily, were distributed as presents from their "not so secret Santa." On Christmas Eve he would personally greet cabbies who were lined up in their taxis in front of his Lexington Hotel headquarters. Wishing them a hearty "Buon Natale, Merry Christmas", he would give each of them $50 in gratitude for their having steered customers to his speakeasies.

Gambling was one of the Big Fella's favorite recreational outlets. Unlike many of his contemporaries, Capone insisted that the games at his establishments be strictly "on-the-level". The odds were always in the favor of the house anyway, so why be greedy and cheat the public? He personally liked to follow horse racing. The only problem was that the horses he followed usually ended up following all the other horses. Rumor has it that he lost about a million dollars a year at various racetracks around the country. When the ponies weren't running there was the dog racing at the Hawthorne Kennel Club in Cicero, which Capone opened in partnership with George "Bugs" Moran prior to their relationship going completely to the dogs.

Big Al goes fishing.

Chapter 14

The Crash of 1929

With the arrival of 1929, things seemed to turn abruptly sour in Chicago's gangland. The winter was unusually hard and bitter weather-wise and otherwise. Prices and demand were up, but whisky inventories were way down, especially for Moran's northsiders. This tension within the market led Moran to order his guys to hijack some of Al Capone's whisky trucks. Additionally, control of the alky cookers on the west side was particularly coveted by all parties. The relatively bad quality of their product could be tolerated in view of the prevailing market conditions. Whoever controlled the presidency of the Sicilian Union had (as always) unfettered access to that vast stock of booze.

Al made the wise decision to go south for the winter. He and his family retreated to their Palm Island compound where they could enjoy the warm sunshine, tropical breezes and sanctuary that was far removed from the tense, gritty, dangerous Chicago City streets. Capone could still make major decisions then relay them by telephone to "Greasy Thumb"

Joey Aiello

Pasqualioro Lolardo

Tony Lombardo

Guzik and Frank "The Enforcer" Nitti. The heavy lifting could always be entrusted to "Machine Gun" Jack McGurn, **Louie "Little New York" Capmagna** and **Tony "Joe Batters" Accardo.** Al was one of the first to pioneer the practice of "telecommuting to work".

The first matter that demanded his attention during his extended absence from Chicago was the opening for the office of president of the Sicilian Union. The vacancy had occurred following the daring, daylight assassination of **Tony "The Mafia King" Lombardo**, who was gunned down in the Chicago Loop in the middle of a rush hour crowd. There was little doubt that the hit was engineered by **Joey Aiello,** a Moran ally who had a burning desire to personally head the *Unione Siciliana.* Added to the mix was the strong suspicion that Joseph Lolardo, the bodyguard of the deceased, was set up his own boss. By the way, Lolardo was a Capone ally, just for good measure.

The stewpot of a plot thickened even more. To the dismay of the ambitious Mr. Aiello, the newly elected President of the Sicilian Union was...**Pasqualioro "Patsy" Lolardo** a Capone ally and the brother of Joseph Lolardo who had killed Tony Lombardo. Whew! It was now getting hard to keep track of the players, even with a scorecard. So, to briefly recap: Joey (who was Patsy's brother) shot Tony (who was the pal of the other Joey) and then Patsy became President instead of the other Joey who had been pal of Tony who got shot, O.K.?

Late on the afternoon of January 2, 1929 Mr. and Mrs. Pasqualioro "Patsy" Lolardo returned home from a shopping trip to downtown Chicago. Shortly thereafter, three unannounced visitors arrived. Mrs. Lolardo set out wine and snacks, then left to go to another room to do some ironing. Within an hour she was a widow. Patsy's hospitality had been repaid by bullets in his own front parlor. Even though Mrs. Lolardo identified Joey Aiello's mugshot as one of the three visitors to their home that afternoon, he was never brought to trial. This was yet another unsolved case that would ultimately be resolved by "street justice".

The grisly aftermath of the St. Valentine's Day Massacre.

Chapter 15

Unhappy Valentine's Day

Perhaps the plans for the complete annihilation of the "Bugs" Moran gang had already been set in motion prior to the murder of "Patsy" Lolardo. In retrospect, it does seem noteworthy that telephone records showed an unusually high volume of calls from Jack

McGurn to Capone's Florida retreat in the days between the first week of January and the thirteenth day of February, halting abruptly on that day. Maybe the guys just missed each other's company.

Louise Rolfe was "Machine Gun" Jack McGurn's blonde alibi.

Uncorroborated rumors over the years set forth an elaborate scenario incorporating the active participation of the "Purple Gang" of Detroit headed up by "Dizzy", "Izzy" and "Rizzy" Bernstein. The conjecture was due to the amicable business relationship between them and Capone relating to the importation of Canadian whisky from across the border bounded by the shallow Detroit River. Legend has it that "Bugs" Moran had received a surprise overture from the Bernstein boys, offering premium whisky at a discount price due to overstock on their end.

Supposedly, a rendezvous had been arranged at Moran's S.M.C. Cartage Company headquarters at 2122 North Clark Street at 10:30 a.m. on Valentine's Day. This appointment would pinpoint Moran's location and line him up in the crosshairs of would-be-assassins. This maneuver may have been one of the elements in the planning of the operation. The guerilla warfare tactics of setting up an ambush fell well within the expertise of these hit-and-run assailants.

Circumstantial connection was later made between two streetfront, second floor apartments several buildings apart on the opposite side of the street from the garage. It seemed odd to discover that a room was rented at 2119 North Clark Street on the same day that a room was rented at 2135 North Clark Street, both paid for a month in advance, both having views of the front door of the S.M.C. Cartage company from opposite directions, and both vacated without notice after only a week on the morning of February 14, 1929. Moran's arrival could be viewed from whichever direction he headed that morning. If Moran was punctual for once, then everything would fall into place as planned. The lookouts would call the firing squad who would then drive over, bump everybody off according to script, and exit offstage.

During the course of the morning, one-by-one, Moran's crew arrived at the garage: the brothers Gusenberg (Frank and Pete); James Clark and Adam Heyer (prominent local bootleggers); John May (the truck mechanic at the garage); and Al Weinshank (a speakeasy operator who doubled as the treasurer of the outfit) accompanied by his German Shepard companion, "Highball". The lookouts across the way had only to await the arrival of a seventh man, George "Bugs" Moran himself. They could then alert the players waiting in the wings disguised as policemen, who would come right over as the lookouts would then abandon their posts. Sure enough, unlucky number seven arrived shortly, dressed in brown head-to-toe as Moran always was and otherwise fitting his physical descriptions. What a surprise it must have been to later discover that they had mistaken the identity of a hapless optician for that of "Scarface" Al Capone's chief nemesis! Dr. Reinhart Schwimmer, a local optician who liked to visit with the boys and listen to their stories as they played cards, picked a bad day to make a social call. Mistaken for Moran, he would later receive the treatment intended for him. Some days it just doesn't pay to get up.

Among the dead were brothers **Frank and Peter Gusenberg**, Moran-enforcers who had ambushed Jack McGurn on two separate occasions in 1928 (the first time so severely

No one was ever convicted for the St. Valentine's Day Massacre that left seven dead.

Capone rival "Bugs" Moran was down with the sniffles during the St. Valentine's Day Massacre.

wounding him he was hospitalized for three weeks).

At 10:55 a.m., two blocks from the garage, a newspaper delivery truck sideswiped a police car. The newsie later told investigators that he was relieved and astounded when the occupants of the squad car merely waved him off and continued on their way. Moments later, a local youth observed a police squad car with a damaged fender slide into a parking space in front of the garage. Four men got out. All four were carrying what appeared to be long boxes. Two men were in Chicago Police Department uniforms complete with badges. The other two men wore suits, ties, overcoats and fedoras. The young man was excited at the prospect of observing close up the real, live arrest of some criminals. The driver of the vehicle remained behind the wheel. He was a tough looking character who told the kid in no uncertain terms to beat it out of there. He did as he was told. However, he merely ducked out of sight in a nearby doorway.

Shortly thereafter, the chill morning air was punctured by the deep rumble of machine gun fire from inside the building, followed by two shotgun blasts! Within seconds, the two men in civilian attire exited the building with their heads down and their hands up. The two uniformed policemen had what looked to be the fabled Thompson submachine guns planted firmly in their suspects' backs as they shoved them into the backseat, entered the vehicle on either side of the "arrestees" and calmly drove away south on Clark Street.

A neighbor lady had heard the commotion. She rushed downstairs, peered through the front window of the garage office only to have her view stopped by the wall separating the office from the garage area itself. A gentleman pedestrian happened by. She asked him to please go in to see if anything was amiss and to check on the welfare of a dog that was inside barking nonstop. He entered the building only to make a hasty exit and exclaim,

36th District C. O. #42 March 28th, 1929

Death: Peter Gusenberg, 434 Roscoe St. 40 years, American, no occupation
Frank Gusenberg, 2138 Lincoln Park, west, 36 years, American, no occupation, married.
John May, 1249 W. Madison St. 35 years, American, mechanic, married
Adam Heyer, 2024 Farragut St. 40 years, American, accountant, married.
Albert Weinshenk, 6320 Kenmore Av. 26 years, American, cleaner and dyer, married.
Albert Kachellek, alias James Clark, 40 years, German, no occupation, married. 6036 Gunnison
Reinhardt Schwimmer, 2100 Lincoln Park, west, 29 years, American, optometrist, single.

Time of Death: Frank Gusenberg, 1.30 p.m. Febr. 14, 1929
All others at 10.40 a.m. February 14, 1929.

Place of Death: Frank Gusenberg at Alexian Brothers Hospital
All others at 2122 N. Clark St.

Cause of Death: Numerous Bullet Wounds.

Witnesses: Clair Mc Allister, 2124 N. Clark St.
Mrs. Max Landesman, 2124 N. Clark St.
Mrs. Lucy Powell, 1249 W. Madison St.
Phillip May, 1247 W. Madison St.
Josephine Morin, 2125 N. Clark St.
James Wilcox, 614 Vedder St.
Sam Schneider, 2124 N. Clark St.
Elmer Lewis, 311 S. Turner Av.

HISTORY OF CASE: At 10.45 a.m. February 14, 1929 Mrs. Landesman, 2124 N. Clark St. called the station and said there was a shooting in the garage next door at 2122 N. Clark St. Sergeant Thos. J. Loftus, Officers Geo. Love and Thos. Christy of the Auto Detail and Sergeant James Quirk, Squad 31-B, responded and entered the S. M. C. Cartage Co. garage at 2122 N. Clark St. and about half way back in the garage on the north side against the wall they found six men lying dead, shot to death with machine gun bullets. They were on a line with the wall. Peter Gusenberg was the farthest west. He was seated in a chair and hanging over the back. Next to him, lying on the floor, was Albert Weinshenk. They were fully clothed with overcoats and hats. The next on the floor was Adam Heyer, who was the owner of the garage and he was also fully clothed to hat and overcoat. Next to him was John May, 1249 W. Madison St. He was dressed in coveralls. He was a mechanic in this garage. Next to him was Reinhardt Schwimmer, who was fully dressed to overcoat and hat and next to him was James Clark, who was dressed in a suit but no overcoat. About fifteen feet away, crawling towards the front door, was Frank Gusenberg, who said to Sergt. Loftus, "Please take me to a hospital". On the floor near him was a .38 cal. revolver, fully loaded, which later was identified

A copy of a police report from the St. Valentine's Day Massacre. Read this report and more starting on page 95.

Crowds gather outside the SMC Cartage Company on Clark Street.

"That garage is full of dead men!"

The police were summoned and arrived within ten minutes to a scene of horror. Six men were lying in a bloody, gruesome heap at the base of the north wall. A trail of blood led to the prone figure of Frank Gusenberg who was trying to make a getaway. His prognosis was not rosy! As a matter of fact, he died only three hours later. He had made no death bed confession or accusation, staying true to the gangland code of "omerta", an ancient Sicilian expression for keeping silent to authorities. Even as the end was near, he would only say, "Nobody shot me. I ain't shot!"

The only survivor was "Highball', the dog who had entered with Mr. Weinshank and been tethered to the bumper of a truck where he had managed to avoid a ricochet bullet. The young fella who had observed the killers both entering and exiting the building volunteered to assist the investigators by going through mug shots. He positively identified

“Machine Gun” Jack McGurn, John Scalise and **Fred “Killer” Burke,** a killer-for-hire from St. Louis.

The newspaper headlines on February 15, 1929, screamed, “Doctor Slain In Massacre.” Rather than explaining the carnage on Clark Street as simply an amped up gangland hit, the press figured that the public would identify more closely with the disaster if a “Civilian” was an innocent victim. Never mind that “Doc” Schwimmer wasn’t really an optometrist but was only an optician in a retail shop who fitted “cheaters” onto customers. Newspapers sell most readily when the headlines are sensational and compelling, regardless of the degree to which the content is factual.

Both McGurn and Scalise were indicted for the St. Valentine’s Day Massacre, but were armed with alibis that got them off the hook. Jack had a “blonde alibi”, **Louise Rolfe.** She insisted that she and Jack had a romantic morning together, far away from the scene on Clark Street. She and McGurn quickly married, thus disarming the prosecution from forcing her to testify against him. Scalise was sheltered by his shadow, Albert Anselmi, who vouched for his companion’s presence at a location miles away.

An all-points bulletin was issued for Mr. Fred Burke. The manhunt proved fruitless for several months, until he was arrested in St. Louis and extradited to Michigan to be tried for the murder of a St. Joseph, Michigan policeman following a traffic altercation. He did a life sentence in that state and died in prison never having admitted his guilt in the Massacre.

No one was ever convicted for the St. Valentine’s Day Massacre. One of the lookouts snitched years later that the gunmen were Burke and Fred Goetz, Gus Winkler and Murray “The Camel” Humphreys. Goetz and Winkler were killed in shootouts. Humphreys got sent up on a tax rap in ’30, coming back to Chicago five years later as a hot shot in what had once been the Capone mob.

“Bugs” Moran had been spared being splattered against the wall of the garage by a case of influenza that kept him in bed that morning. His initial reply to reporters begging for his comment on the story was, “You must be new in town, kid. Only Al Capone kills like that!”

Capone was out of town with an ironclad alibi. This was always the case whenever there was a special event of this nature. At the time of the Massacre, Capone was entertaining prize fighter Jack Sharky and the Dade County, Florida Solicitor at his Palm Island home. When informed of the events of that morning, he issued this statement: “It was tragic what happened up there in Chicago. That guy ‘Bugs’ Moran is nuts. That’s why they call him ‘Bugs’. I’m out of town attending to business, and he lines his own guys up against a wall and shoots them all. Some of those guys were personal friends of mine.” As usual, the most lavish wreaths of roses at the funerals had cards that were signed, “From your Pal, Al”.

John Scalise (left) and Albert Anselmi

Chapter 16

A Dinner Invitation

Mr. Capone spent the remainder of the winter and early spring in Florida, entrusting his affairs in Chicago to his trusted lieutenants. Not everyone proved to be completely trustworthy in his absence. John Scalise and Albert Anselmi plotted treason. They had concocted a plan to assassinate the Boss and then install a goofball named Joseph "Hoptoad" Guinta as President of the Sicilian Union. The clandestine plot never came to fruition. Once their scheme had been discovered, Capone returned to Chicago to dispose of the traitors.

The motion picture version of this exercise in conflict resolution features a lavish banquet after which Al performs a soliloquy in which baseball is praised as a metaphor for team work. Extending the metaphor into an object lesson, the craniums of Scalise, Anselmi and Giunta are used as baseballs for Capone's home runs! More likely what happened was yet another instance of "Machine Gun" Jack McGurn literally exercising overkill. Bear in mind that this trio of traitors was not only Sicilian, but also they were the genuine article "old country Mafioso". Capone might get away with ordering their disposal, but there was no reason for him to "take out the garbage" himself. Vincenzo Gibaldi a/k/a Jack McGurn was basically the antithesis of the Mafioso, who clung together and preferred to shoot their prey from behind. He was independent, confrontational and met his victims face-to-face whenever possible. Born in Licata, Sicily in 1903, he could, at least, deflect the

Scalise and Anselmi on the way to court.

criticism that he was not their paisan (country man).

The infamous "dinner party" occurred on May 8, 1929 in Cicero. According to one of the guests who later confided to a reporter, the "host" (Jack McGurn) tied Scalise, Anselmi and Giunta to their chair backs, beat them to a pulp with his fists, shot them, and threw their corpses into a truck. After a short ride, they were deposited into the Douglas Park Lagoon on the west side of Chicago. The bodies floated to the surface the following day to the stunned surprise of some fishermen.

Al was summoned to an impromptu conference in Atlantic City that was to be attended by Johnny Torrio, Charley "Lucky" Luciano, "Bugs" Moran, several of the New York syndicate bosses, and himself. Al Capone and his longtime bodyguard, Frankie Rio, boarded the train at Chicago's Union Station on May 10, en route to a meeting that portended his descent down a slippery slope that would lead to his ultimate demise. The general consensus was that the triple murder of Scalise, Anselmi and Guinta, following so closely on the heels of the St. Valentine's Massacre, could easily become a firestorm of unimaginable proportions.

The Massacre had generated negative publicity throughout the world. Outside of an actual military operation, no one could recall a slaughter of this magnitude ever occurring. What was going on in Chicago? What was planned for the second half of 1929? Had Capone really gone out of his mind, drunk with power? The poor fellas in the garage were relative unknowns, but that was not the case with the three Sicilians. John Scalise was a high-ranking member of the national commission of the Sicilian Union, not just some anonymous Mafia soldier. This was very serious business, indeed. It was serious enough for Johnny Torrio, who by now was the acknowledged "Godfather of Modern Day Organized Crime", to advise that Alphonse Capone should take a sabbatical to reflect upon his personal management style.

On the afternoon of May 13, 1929, Al Capone and Frankie Rio were arrested on the railway platform in Philadelphia, Pennsylvania just prior to boarding the westbound train for Chicago. A policeman thought that he recognized the big fella with the prominent scars on his left check from newspapers or magazines or somewhere! The big guy answered the cop's inquiry regarding his identity, "Hiya, pal, I'm Al Capone." The policeman couldn't help but notice the shoulder holster and gun barely concealed inside the gentleman's suit coat. It was almost as if he wanted to be arrested! Al and Frankie were, in fact, arrested on charges of carrying concealed weapons. No one really noted that Frankie got little more than a slap on the wrist. The entire English speaking world would soon read in the daily papers that Al Capone was sentenced to nine months in the Eastern State Penitentiary in Philadelphia on a charge that normally netted offenders about ninety days in the can! It was during this extended absence that the wheels were set in motion that would guarantee an end to the reign of Scarface.

The Untouchables were led by Eliot Ness (back row, right).

Chapter 17

Enter The Untouchables

In 1929, a group of prominent, wealthy Chicago civic leaders (including social activist Jane Addams and Colonel Robert McCormick, publisher of the *Chicago Tribune)* formed a private investigatory organization. This group was known as The Secret Six, since they sought the shield of anonymity to protect them from those who they sought to investigate. They prevailed upon President Herbert Hoover to focus federal attention upon the Capone criminal enterprise in Chicago. The responsibility of enforcing Prohibition had recently been transferred from the Treasury Department to the Justice Department. This armed

Agents confiscate bootleg liquor.

its agents with more law enforcement officers with experience in dealing with cases that could ultimately lead to criminal prosecution.

A special operation was authorized for Chicago. It would be headed up by a twenty-six-year-old native southsider who had graduated in 1925 with an accounting degree from the University of Chicago. That degree had facilitated him getting hired as a Treasury Agent, but it hadn't exactly equipped young **Eliot Ness** for his initial assignment as a Prohibition Agent. A map, a compass and prior experience as a hunter would have come in handy.

Ness's first position had been in South Carolina. Shooting at "revenooers" with their squirrel guns seemed to be the favorite pastime of the hillbillies in the backwoods…and they were real good at it, too! Ness had been seriously considering other employment when his brother-in-law, a prohibition agent in Chicago, was able to arrange for him to be reassigned to the "windy city". This saved Eliot Ness from reapplying for his old job as an insurance investigator, which he held for two years following his college days.

Ness was allowed the opportunity of hiring his own squad of incorruptible agents who would be on call seven days a week to assist him in this major assignment: to bring down Al Capone. The agents all were selected from the ranks of Civil Service workers and were educated, diligent and fastidiously honest. Initially, the focus was on destroying the breweries, alky cooking plants and other Prohibition offshoots, such as gambling dens that were fueled by the revenue from alcohol operations.

Bootleg girls hid illegal libations in containers covered by their skirts.

A succession of successful raids in Chicago Heights was followed by high profile raids on breweries in Cicero, the south side of Chicago, and the industrial corridor on the north side known as Goose Island.

The officers under Ness's command worked skillfully as undercover detectives in discovering the details of the operations that they would bust. The element of surprise enabled them to conduct raids with a minimum of gunplay and excessive force. Informants were utilized as snitches in exchange for leniency in pending criminal cases. Without the assistance of these informants, there would have been little hope of determining the exact locations of underground bootlegging plants among the labyrinth of Chicago's vast industrial areas. The smells generated by factories, tanneries, and the stockyards provided olfactory camouflage for the odorous breweries and distilleries.

Ness's assignment was eased somewhat by Capone being incarcerated in Pennsylvania on his concealed weapon rap. The successes of Ness and his agents had the two-fold effect of reducing the profits of the Capone organization while generating positive publicity for the "good guys" who were fighting a prolonged losing streak! Finally, there seemed to be something to embellish the reputation of the law enforcement community. The well-publicized raids by seemingly incorruptible coppers inspired the creative writing skills of a local reporter who claimed that one of the arrested gangsters remarked in amazement, "These guys won't take bribes. They are untouchable!" True or not, the label stuck to these agents who struggled by on $2,500 a year in an era when the bootleggers would have gladly paid them ten times that amount to lay off!

A potent combination of "The Untouchable" Treasury agents, local police and the Internal Revenue Service was poised to deliver the knockout blow to "the Big Fella". An IRS agent named Frank Wilson began putting the puzzle pieces together. Over the years, various police raids had been made upon the gambling houses run by the mob. During these raids evidence, both physical and anecdotal, was amassed. Subsequent investigations revealed that Capone had seventeen different bank accounts. That evidence along with his well-known visits to racetracks and spendthrift habits cumulatively proved to be his Achilles heel when he was tried for income tax evasion several years later.

The "Big Guy" was released from the Eastern State Penitentiary in the spring of 1930. A sense of desperation permeated his operations. Public momentum was gaining for the repeal of the Volstead Act of Prohibition. Politicians were running campaigns with the slogan, "Peace, Prosperity and Repeal of Prohibition!" Once the Eighteenth Amendment was revoked, the gravy train would be derailed.

Police raids on speakeasies and bawdy houses were happening almost daily. Rumors abounded that employees of some of the gambling joints were going state's evidence to avoid prosecution. To compound everything else, the stock market crash of October 1929 had pulled the plug on the economy. The gains made during the Roaring Twenties seemed to be going down the drain in a rush.

Desperate times can sometimes incite ill-advised, desperate measures. There had always been an unwritten rule in Chicago's underworld that there were two classes of people you didn't harm: Catholic priests and newspaper reporters. The former group was exempted because the overwhelming majority of the gangsters were "cradle Catholics". Mostly of Irish, Polish, Italian ancestry, they were culturally Catholic by personal identification (if not in actual religious practice). At the very least, they assumed that it would be very unlucky to shoot a man of the cloth.

The latter group got a pass because nobody wanted bad publicity on top of all their other troubles. Heaven forbid, lest anyone should think that these bootleggers were bad guys!

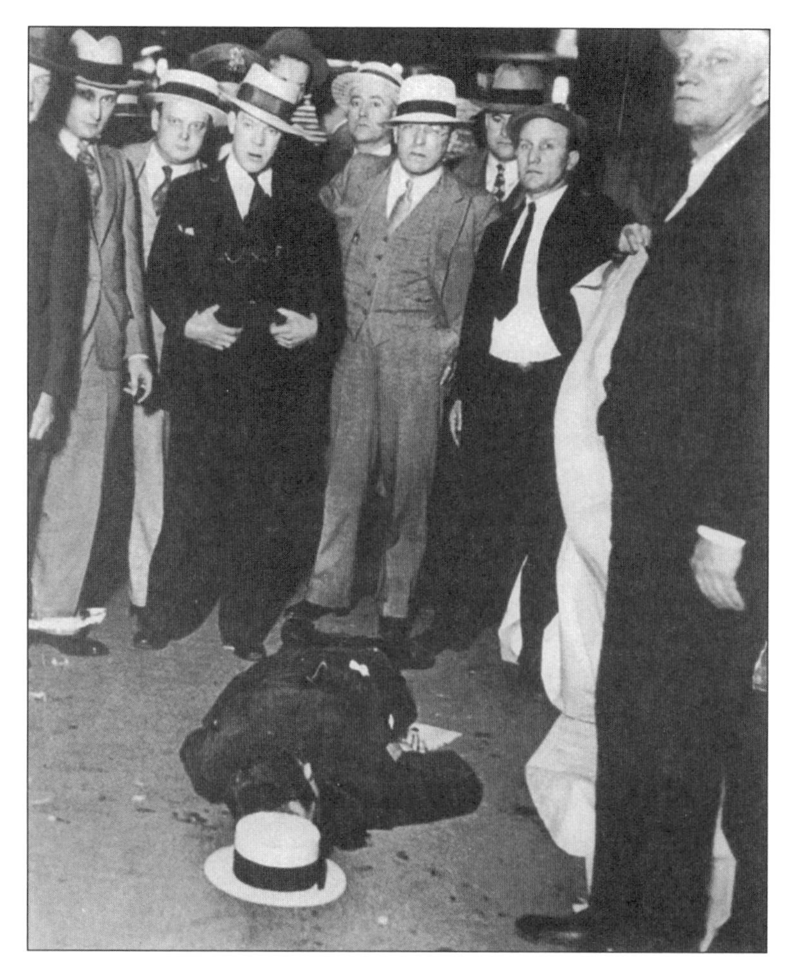
Newspaperman Alfred "Jake" Lingle was gunned down in broad daylight.

Chapter 18

Truth & Justice

The clergy made it through Prohibition unscathed, but the press did suffer a major casualty. A reporter named **Alfred "Jake" Lingle** was gunned down during rush hour in the pedestrian underpass to the rail station at Michigan Avenue and Randolph Street, just downstairs from the Library. Lingle wrote a daily crime beat column for the Chicago Tribune, following the day-to-day actions of the Chicago Police Department in the thrilling pursuit of murderers, robbers and gangsters. He was well suited to the task, especially since he was a life long friend of Police Commissioner Russell. This association had given Lingle the opportunity to become a confidant of every captain, detective and beat cop at every stationhouse in the city. They all fed him the inside dope in the hope of someday getting a mention for their heroic deeds. When Jake was gunned down in broad daylight on June 9, 1930, it seemed that the entire city -- policemen, and civilians alike -- was up in arms!

The funeral of Jake Lingle outdid anything that had preceded it. It was even bigger than the most ostentatious gangster funerals. It seemed that every policeman on the force was in attendance, along with every politician and school boy! The different newspaper publishers, in a rare display of unity, offered a twenty five thousand dollar reward for information leading to the capture of the perpetrators of this heinous crime! Their underlying hope was that the trail would somehow ultimately lead to the doorstep of Alphonse Capone.

The crescendo for justice reached a deafening pitch, only to be deflated like a helium-filled balloon several weeks later. Certain information came to light from undisclosed sources. It seemed as though Mr. Lingle would have been stellar in the field of offering financial advice to the readers of the Tribune. He seemed remarkably adept at stretching the dollar. On a salary of $65 a week he was able to afford a comfortable home for his family in Chicago, a lakefront home in Indiana on Lake Michigan, and luxury vacations for himself and his wife, frequent trips to the racetracks where he was notoriously unlucky. He also managed to accumulate $100,000 in his bank account. How did he ever do that making a measly sixty five bucks a week?

Jake Lingle had supplemented his income by selling information to the bootleggers that was very useful in their efforts. His cost-saving intelligence was valuable enough that they freely expressed their gratitude to him in a financially remunerative way. In other words, "he was on the take!"

Specific advance intelligence was made available for a price. This info gave the criminals ample notice of raids, thereby avoiding arrest and also allowing the opportunity to relocate operations whenever possible. Apparently, Lingle had been working both sides of the fence. His downfall had been to become greedy and unreasonably demanding. The mob doesn't mind paying a fair price for value received (if absolutely necessary), but the line is drawn when the payoff becomes a shakedown. The word on the street was that Jake was playing one gang against the other while demanding ever-increasing payments for his consultation. The gambler finally overplayed his hand. His bluff was called. He was busted.

To get the heat off him, Capone designated a low level thug, Leo Vincent Brothers, to be the outifit scapegoat. Brothers took the rap for the boys by doing a three-year stretch in Stateville Prison in Joliet.

Times were definitely changing. When Capone and McGurn attended a Northwestern University football game in the fall of 1930, they were booed and pelted with debris. The two were humiliated and beat it out of there through the nearest exit! This was a far cry from the cheers that they had enjoyed only two years earlier when they were greeted as hometown heroes.

Nobody ever said that Al Capone couldn't take a hint. He was content to go into retirement. He enjoyed the climate, social scene, and deep sea fishing in Florida. Mae and Sonny wouldn't miss the pressure and danger of Chicago any more than he would. If it was only that easy! He wasn't an ordinary pensioner who could gracefully exit his humdrum job to enjoy himself while idling away his time. He would always be a wanted man with a lifetime of accumulated enemies, not the least of whom was Uncle Sam.

Jake Lingle

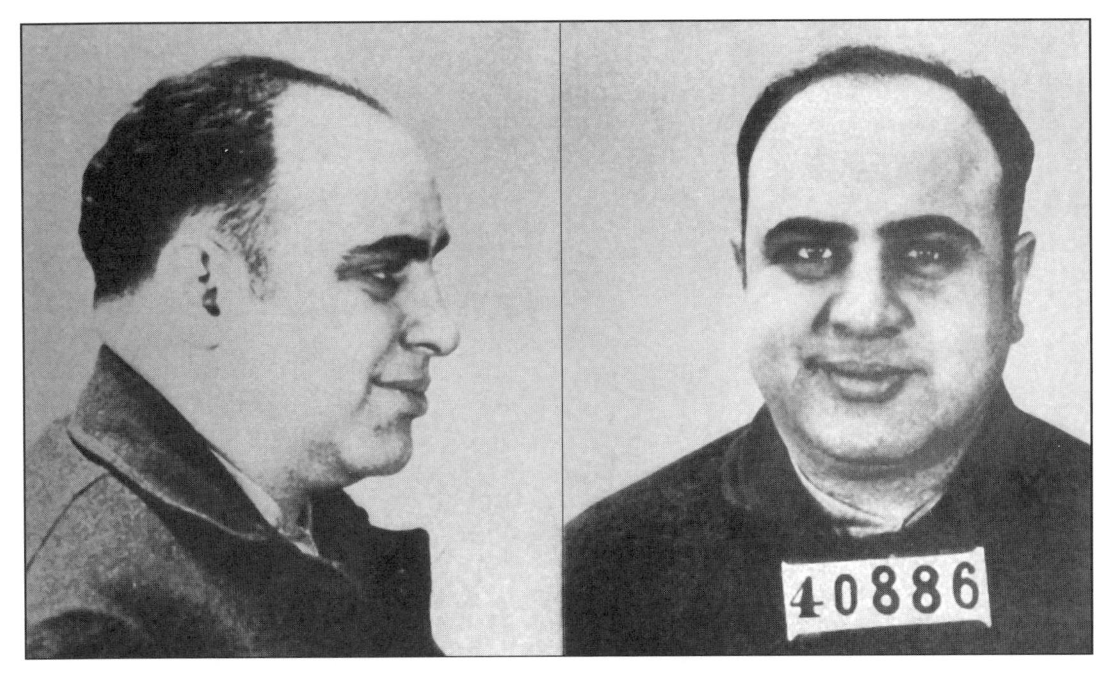

Big Al smiles for the camera in his Alcatraz mug shot.

Chapter 19

Death & Taxes

By 1931, the government had amassed enough evidence to bring Alphonse Capone to trial for income tax evasion! He was summoned to appear before the Federal Court of the Northern District of Illinois. The charge was failing to report approximately one million dollars income, for which the tax liability would be $210,000. As his attorneys were attempting to negotiate a plea, Al went fishing in the Bahamas. He had a doctor write a note stating that he was too ill to travel for his court date. When photographs surfaced showing him in pajamas and bathrobe smiling while fishing off the stern of a yacht, he earned a contempt-of-court citation that was subsequently tacked on to his sentence for tax evasion.

Despite a pretrial agreement to pay the tax bill in lieu of incarceration, Capone was fined $50,000 and sentenced to eleven years in prison. He sat in the Cook County Jail for six months for his contempt-of-court charge before boarding the train for the federal penitentiary in Atlanta, Georgia.

TREASURY DEPARTMENT
Internal Revenue Service

Intelligence Unit
Chicago

Chicago, Illinois,
July 8, 1931.

WCH-MD

CONFIDENTIAL

Internal Revenue Agent in Charge,
Chicago, Illinois.

In re Alphonse Capone,
7244 Prairie Avenue,
Chicago, Illinois.

Alphonse Capone is, without a doubt, the best advertised and most talked of gangster in the United States today. Reams and reams of newsprint and magazine paper has been used up in exploiting Al. Capone as the "Big Shot" in his various activities as the boss of the so-called Cicero syndicate which carried on a very lucrative business in manufacturing and selling beer and alcohol, operating gambling houses, and houses of prostitution.

Al Capone has been mentioned in connection with practically every major crime committed in Chicago within the last few years; possibly some of the stories are true, but, no doubt, a great deal of the stuff printed originated in the fertile brow of some newspaper reporter or magazine writer.

Al Capone, a punk hoodlum, came to Chicago from New York about 1920, as a protege of John Torrio, who, at the time was a lieutenant of Jim Colisimo. The first heard of Capone was as a bouncer in a notoriously tough joint called the "Four Deuces". In the course of time, Colisimo, following the path of all good gangsters, was "bumped off", and Torrio took control. True to tradition, the guns again began to blaze, but this time the person behind the gun evidently had poor eyesight and Torrio, instead of going to the

Internal Revenue agents documented their case against Al Capone in this letter. Their investigation led to Capone's being found guilty of tax evasion and jailed at Alcatraz. Read the complete letter on page 102.

Money cannot buy everything, but it bought Mr. Capone various amenities in prison in Atlanta. He enjoyed a carpeted, private cell with original oil paintings on the walls. His meals were catered affairs, with the food brought in from the finest restaurants in the city. He wore suits and ties instead of prison garb. To facilitate communication with the outside world, he had a radio, a telephone, and a tickertape machine. All of these details were noted by a reporter who made a visit to give an account of how Al Capone was suffering through his imprisonment. When news surfaced regarding his preferential treatment, the warden was taken to task while a transfer was arranged.

In 1934, a new facility was opened to house the most dangerous, notorious, high profile inmates within the prison system. This island retreat for criminal elite in the middle of San Francisco Bay was, of course, Alcatraz Island. There was only one way onto "the Rock" and one way off. The short boat ride across the cold, choppy waters of the bay may as well have been across the ocean. The divide between the city of San Francisco with its teeming, diverse population and legendary nightlife contrasted with the stark reality of Alcatraz as night differs from day.

It was a rude awakening for the handcuffed former big shot when he exited the launch and greeted the first guard he encountered with his usual "Hi, pal, I'm Al Capone!" His salutation was rebuffed by a steely eyed guard who said, "No, here you are number 0087!" As the guard slammed the heavy steel door behind him, reality quickly set in. A concrete room furnished with only a toilet, sink and steel rack with a paper thin mattress for a bed was Capone's address for now.

The "Big Guy" had been cut down to size. He tried to make the best of a bad situation. His job in the prison laundry helped to pass the time between the monthly visits from his wife, Mae. The routine was rudely interrupted when another inmate didn't like the way that Al was folding laundry. The guy shanked him with a pair of scissors. The injury was sufficient to earn Al a stay in the prison infirmary for several weeks, after which he was reassigned to a floor washing detail.

While recovering from his injuries, Al began to exhibit the recurring symptoms of syphilis that had first surfaced years prior. He had a morbid fear of hypodermic needles. Paranoid that a doctor might be bribed to inject him with poison, Capone refused injections of medicine that may have cured him. Various alternative treatments had failed and his condition was rapidly worsening. His skin was becoming blotchy and his thinking muddled as the disease entered his brain.

In 1939, he was diagnosed with paresis of the brain. The blood vessels of his brain expanded and contracted, leading him to wander into and out of reality. So far had the former "King of Crime" fallen from his throne that the young prisoners openly detested him. A relic from the "old days of Prohibition," they rudely called him the "Wop With a Mop!" His health had deteriorated so badly he was considered unfit for imprisonment. No longer a threat to anyone, he was transferred to a hospital in Baltimore that specialized in the treatment of venereal diseases, but after a year it was determined that his condition was terminal.

Returning to Chicago was not an option. The Palm Island, Florida home was the family sanctuary. Mae was the supportive wife that she had always been, despite Al's quite obvious sexual transgressions in years prior. Young Sonny transferred from Notre Dame University to the University of Miami after his freshman year to assist in taking care of his father.

Eight years passed before Al finally succumbed to his illness on January 25, 1947, at the age of forty eight. He was returned to Chicago to be buried in the family plot in Mount Olivet Cemetery on the city's south side. Unfortunately, the gravesite was frequently vandalized by drunks and souvenir hunters, necessitating the need for reburial elsewhere.

The remains of Al, along with those of his mother, father, sisters and brothers, found their finally nesting place in Mount Carmel Cemetery in the suburb of Hillside, Illinois. There, in an obscure back space with a hedge shielding the family name below the large, but simple granite cross is the burial spot of the "Big Fella". At the head of a well-worn grave site is a marble stone that bears the humble inscription:

ALPHONSE CAPONE

1899-1947

MY JESUS, MERCY

REPRINT BROUGHT TO YOU BY M-C ASSOCIATES

War Near in Europe! Hillman's Amazing Revelations Start Today

$2.50

Turn to Page 4

Herald and Chicago Examiner

METROPOLITAN EDITION

PRICE 3 CENTS

WEDNESDAY, DECEMBER 6, 1933

Telephone Randolph 2121

TWO PARTS

PROHIBITION ERA ENDED!

LOOP CROWDS HAIL REPEAL

Final Vote; ion Follows

Groups of Girls Line up at el Bars.

U.S. STUDIES 'FAVORITISM' IN HOME LOANS

Order Extradition of Touhy Gang for Factor Trial Here

NATIONAL CITY BANK FOR U MONEY

Post Mortem Prohibition

The repeal of Prohibition on December 5, 1933 signaled the end of an era that can justifiably be regarded as the "Golden Age of Organized Crime." Previously regarded by many as public benefactors, providing goods and services that should never have been deemed illegal in the first place, these same individuals became public menaces once they moved into other arenas.

Unemployed thugs provided muscle that led to the undue influence of organized crime in the worlds of trade unions, various industries, and politics. Their bosses were forced by circumstances to engage in more sophisticated types of criminal activities, for which many of them were ill-equipped. While we certainly do not suffer under the delusion that these wild, unruly men were admirable or chivalrous, they were, by-and-large, more ordinary than eccentric and more impulsive than sadistic. Regardless of everything – good or bad – that resulted from their wild and violent ways, they definitely put the roar into the Roaring Twenties.

The Survivors

Tony "Joe Batters" Accardo ascended to the role of kingpin in 1945. He ruled the roost for twenty years, leading the charge into Las Vegas with its numerous enticements. After leaving the daily grind to his subordinates, Accardo still made the big life and death decisions. He died peacefully in 1992 at age 86, having never spent a night in the hospital during his entire life.

Fred "Killer" Burke successfully avoided prosecution for his role in the St. Valentine's Day Massacre, but spent the last nine years of his life in a Michigan prison for having killed a policeman. Burke died in 1940 at the age of 47 – a morbidly obese diabetic.

Albert Francis "Sonny" Capone, the son of Big Al and Mae, married his high school sweetheart, with whom he fathered four daughters. For a few years, Sonny and his mother operated a restaurant in Miami. He later became a car salesman. Perhaps to avoid the unending notoriety attendant with his surname, Sonny legally changed his name to Albert Francis Brown in 1966. Retiring with his bride to California, he died in 2004 at the age of 87.

Mary Josephine "Mae" Capone was a drop-dead gorgeous and elegant lady. She performed beautifully as the leading lady in the drama of a man who was frequently a bad actor. Widowed in her middle age, it was rumored that the Outfit took care of her and Sonny out of respect for her husband's accomplishments. Mae passed away at age 89 in 1986. Perhaps it is insignificant, but it is nevertheless curious that her remains do not reside next to those of Al Capone in Mount Carmel Cemetery.

The ruins of the Coliseum where Bathhouse Coughlin and Hinky Dink Kenna held their 1st Ward bash.

Ralph "Bottles" Capone followed his little brother Al into the prison system for (what else?) income tax evasion. He was never again a big shot. Ultimately, he retired to Wisconsin to run a dance hall and cigarette vending company. He died in 1974 at the age of 80.

John "Bathhouse" Coughlin was outraged at the newspapers only once in his entire life. He had never expressed outrage at their harsh reviews of his poetic endeavors, nor multiple instances of graft. He did, however, demand a retraction when it was mistakenly reported that he was born in Waukegan, Illinois. He was born in Chicago, and died there in 1938 at the age of 78.

Jake "Greasy Thumb" Guzik was the only man that Al Capone really trusted in business matters. A testimonial to Jake's expertise and integrity is the fact that he remained chief financial officer for the Mob until his death at age 69 in 1956.

Murray "The Camel" Humphreys continued in the role of chief political and labor racketeer for the Outfit, just as he had done during Prohibition. He stuck to his cruel philosophy that, "Any time you become weak, you might as well die," until he kicked the bucket in 1965. He was 66.

"Machine Gun" Jack McGurn was so "hot" following the St. Valentine's Day Massacre, he became unemployable. After Al Capone's departure to the Atlanta Federal Penitentiary, McGurn quickly fell from grace with Frank Nitti and the Outfit. McGurn became a surly loudmouth and a heavy drinker – habits that made him increasingly more perilous to mob interests. His mental state declined along with his personal finances. He became paranoid, and threatened to let the feds in on some of his inside information about higher up mobsters unless Nitti cut him in on the action. McGurn never got the chance to become a snitch. At approximately 1:00 a.m. on February 15, 1936 he was gunned down by "assailants unknown" in a bowling alley at 805 N. Milwaukee

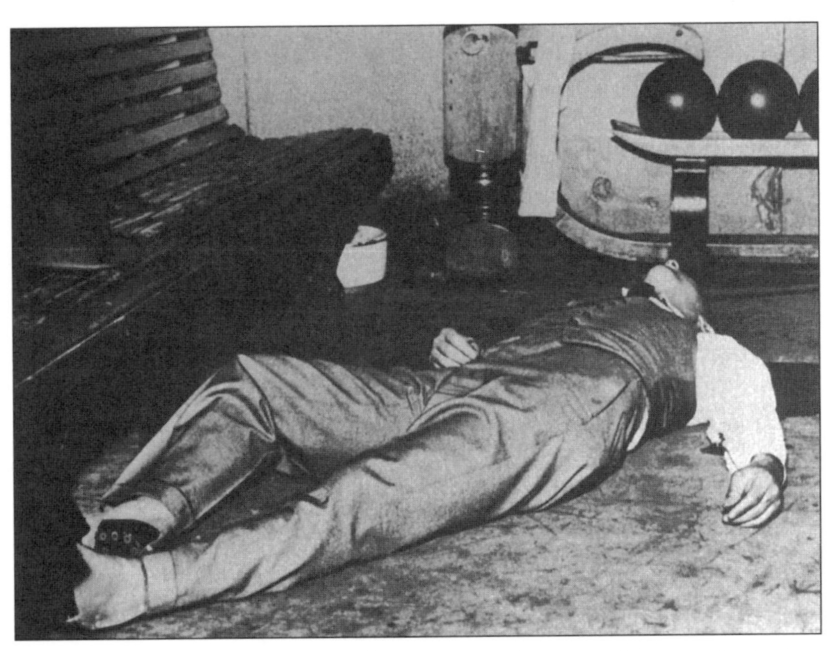

"Machine Gun" Jack McGurn was not spared by the Outfit.

Avenue, Chicago. When the police arrived, the only people still present were the pinsetter and the janitor who had telephoned the police. McGurn's two bowling partners had snatched up the scorecard to conceal their identities. The janitor could only testify that three men had barged in with guns drawn, and told everyone "You move, you die." Three fatal shots were fired into Jack McGurn. A Depression-era greeting card was left at the reception desk (not on his body as most books depict). The card read, "You lost your job, you lost your dough, your jewels, cars and fancy houses; but things could have been worse, you know, you haven't lost your trousers." That summed up the 32-year life of Al Capone's most trusted and feared assassin.

George "Bugs" Moran

George "Bugs" Moran hit the skids after narrowly avoiding being snuffed out in the St. Valentine's Day Massacre. Over the years he was arrested for vagrancy, forgery, and armed robbery. The latter charge earned him a ten-year sentence in the Ohio State Penitentiary. Released in 1956, Bugs Moran moved to Kentucky where he posed as an oil company executive while actually running a bank robbery ring. Eventually he was arrested in Dayton, Ohio for bank robbery -- a federal crime. His conviction led Moran to incarceration at Leavenworth Prison in Kansas, where he died in 1957. He was 65. Despite the vast sums that he had acquired from his "business dealings" during Prohibition, Bugs Moran was buried in a $35 pine coffin in the prison cemetery.

Eliot Ness made his claim to fame by destroying Al Capone's breweries during the waning days of Prohibition. The Internal Revenue Service put Capone in prison with little assistance from Ness received or necessary. Nonetheless, Agent Ness was able to parlay his celebrity into promotions within the Prohibition Bureau and, following Repeal, took the position of Public Safety Director for the City of Cleveland, Ohio, heading up both the police and fire departments. Ness's tenure there was diminished by his failure to solve the serial murders of "The Torso Killer." The well-publicized taunts of the maniac who decapitated hobos and prostitutes in Cleveland's industrial area known as "the Flats," with the accompanying pressure from a terrified public, literally drive Ness to drink. Ironically, the scourge of Chicago's illegal breweries was ruined by a charge of drunken driving that caused a traffic accident. Forced to leave Cleveland, Ness moved to Washington, DC to work for the feds again. Later he became president of a pen company in Pennsylvania. Ness collaborated with writer Oscar Fraley to chronicle a book about his triumphs in Chicago. The book, entitled "The Untouchables," became a hit television series that is still aired in syndication. Sadly, Ness never got to witness the success of his book or the series. He died of a heart attack in 1957 at the age of 75.

Frank "The Enforcer" Nitti fronted as the head of the Outfit following his 1932 release from prison, where he served an eighteen-month stretch for income tax evasion. The confinement had rendered him claustrophobic and terrified of a potential return engagement in the pen. Nitti's later prosecution for racketeering in the motion picture industry led him to commit suicide in 1943 at the relatively young age of 55.

Edward "Spike" O'Donnell became a consultant.

Edward "Spike" O'Donnell gained a measure of respect from "the Establishment" as evidenced by his 1933 appearance before the United States Senate to offer sage advice on how young men could be dissuaded from a life in organized crime if only they were afforded adequate educational and vocational opportunities. O'Donnell had given up on the beer rackets prior to the Repeal of Prohibition, characterizing them as "stupid." Spike was a consultant to both local government and trade unions until his death in 1962 at the age of 72.

Paul "The Waiter" Ricca was the actual head of the Outfit during the first ten years after the repeal of Prohibition. Following a racketeering conviction in 1943, Ricca served three years in prison. Though his prison record prohibited him from associating with mobsters, it did not hinder him from being the final authority in major business transactions and assassinations. When ordering "hits," Ricca would say, "Make him go away." He went away via a heart attack in 1972. He was 69.

Louise "The Blonde Alibi" Rolfe remarried following the death of her husband, "Machine Gun" Jack McGurn. As a matter of fact, she was married six more times – twice to the same gentleman. Adhering to a healthy diet of daiquiris, lobster and Pall Mall cigarettes, the lovely doll lived to be 89. She passed away in Sonoma, California in 1995.

Johhny "The Fox" Torrio retired to New York in 1925 at the age of 43 and with a nestegg of thirty million dollars. He denied any involvement with the underworld, but is generally acknowledged to have been the frequent advisor of Charlie "Lucky" Luciano, Benjamin "Bugsy" Seigel, and Meyer Lansky. In 1957, when he was 75, Johnny The Fox suffered a heart attack while sitting in a Brooklyn barber chair. He held on long enough to die in bed.

Joseph "Polack Joe" Saltis retreated to Wisconsin in 1930, spending an estimated $100,000 building a rustic two-story cedar log cabin lodge and golf course. The Barker Lake Lodge in Hayward, Wisconsin remained Saltis's home until 1947 when he died due to complications from a stomach ulcer.

Thrill seekers congregate outside the SMC Cartage Company after the St. Valentine's Day Massacre.

St. Valentine's Day Massacre Police Documents

The following witness statements and police reports are copied *ver batim* -- typos and all -- from actual documents generated by personnel from the 36th District Husdon Avenue Police who investigated the massacre.

WITNESS STATEMENTS: February 14, 1929

Statement made at the Hudson Ave. Police Station by Mrs. Max Landesman

Q. What is you're name and address? **A.** Mrs. Max Landesman, 2124 N. Clark St., 4th floor.

Q. On February 14, 1929 what if anything occurred at 2122 N. Clark St.?

A. About 10:30 A.M. Feb. 14, 1929, I was ironing in my kitchen when I heard some shots being fired, I ran to the front window and looked out just in time to see a man get into the rear of a large touring car that was facing south on Clark st in front of the garage at 2122 N. Clark St. After the man got into the auto a street car was coming south and it passed this auto and then the machine started away and it passed the southbound street car on the left side and sped south. I then ran downstairs and I looked into the garage door but I could not see anything. I tried the door but it would not open I think it was locked or stuck. I then went back upstairs and asked Mr. McAllister to go downstairs and see if there was anything wrong in the garage and he went downstairs and then came back up and told me to call the police and a doctor that there were some men laying in the garage I then called the police and notified them that there was a shooting at the garage. A few minutes after the police came. Later when the bodies were removed from the garage I spoke to the assistant states attorney and then went down to the States Atty. Office and from there to the Hudson Ave. Station where I am not making this statement and it is all I know about the case and my signature appears below this statement in my own handwriting.

Mrs. Max Landesman
Witnesses
Mrs. Josephine Morin, Clair McAllister, Patrolman. E. A. Erickson, Patrolman A. J. Osterkorn

Statement made at the Hudson Ave. Police Station by Mr. Clair McAllister

Q. What us your name and address? **A**. My name is Clair McAllister and I live at 2124 N. Clark St. on the 2nd floor. I am a contractor that is general sign contractor in business by myself.

Q. What if anything unusual occurred on Feb. 14, 1929?

A. I was in my room at 2124 N. Clark St. when Mrs. Landsman came to me and told me that she heard some shooting downstairs and asked me to go down to the garage and see if there was anything wrong? I went down to the garage next door and pushed open the front door (it was stuck probably on account of being warped or wet) I walked through the office and then into the garage and I smelled something that seemed like there had been some shooting in the place. I also saw smoke in the garage and I looked around and I saw seven men stretched out on the floor and saw blood coming from some of them and then I knew that they were shot. One of the men looked at me and said who is it and I said I just come in to help you out and then I walked right out and told Mrs. Landsman who was up in her flat to call the police and a doctor and told her that there were seven men shot laying in the garage. I waited until the officers came a few minutes later and police wagons took the men away who were shot. Later on I went to the Hudson Ave. Police Station to make this statement that I am now signing. I heard no shooting nor saw anyone leaving the garage where the shooting occurred.

Clair L. McAllister
Witnesses
Patrolman E. A. Erickson, Patrolman A.J. Osterkorn

Statement made at the Hudson Ave. Police Station by Mrs. Josephine Morin
Q. What is your name and address? **A.** My name is Josephine Morin and I live at 2125 N. Clark St. 3rd floor.

Q. Did you witness a shooting on Feb. 14, 1929 about 10:30 A.M.
A. I did not see any shooting.

Q. Do you know anything about a shooting that occurred at 2122 N. Clark st.

A. Yes. About 10:30 A.M. I was looking out the front window of my flat when I saw one or two men coming out of the garage at 2122 N. Clark St. one or two of the men had their hands in the air and were followed by two men in blue uniforms with stars on their coats and the two uniformed men had a gun about 3 feet long in their hands and they all got into a black touring car with side curtains, the car looked like a Cadillac to me and it was parked in front of this garage and was facing south on Clark st. One of the men that had his hands in the air got into the car and got behind the wheel and then the car drove south. I did not notice whether or not the car had a license on it or not. I stayed at the window for a while and then saw some more men come in who machines whom I later found out to be Officers from the Hudson Ave. Station, for I went downstairs to see what all the commotion was about and I heard that six men were shot in the garage at 2122 N. Clark St. Later on some officers came over to my house and asked me to come to the states attorneys office and I went there and from the States Attorneys office I went to the Hudson Ave. Station to make this statement I am now giving and it is all I know about the case and my signature appears below in my own handwriting.

Mrs. Josephine Morin

Witnesses

Mrs. Max Landesman, Clair McAllister, Patrolman E. A. Erickson, Patrolman A.J. Osterkorn

POLICE REPORT: February 18, 1929

From: Ptlmn. J. Connelley and J. Devane, 36th District

To: Captain Commanding 36th District

Subject: 2139 N. Clark St,

1. We interviewed Mrs. Minnie Arvidson, 2051 N. Clark St. Lincoln 8935, proprietress of a rooming house at 2139 N. Clark St. She told us that a man came to her Sunday, January 27th, 1929 and said he wanted a room for his friend and himself (a room each). She said, "Alright, I have 2 rooms at 2139 N. Clark St." He didn't ask to see the rooms then but gave her $1.00 and said "We'll be here tomorrow to pay you the balance and take the rooms." Price was $8.00 each room. Monday afternoon, Jan. 28th, 1929 the other man came and gave her $15.00 which was the balance for two rooms for a week. This man took a front room on the first floor. They told her they were taxi cab drivers and asked her if she had a garage to rent so they could keep their cabs there, but she didn't have any to rent. These were housekeeping rooms and she did not see any of their activities, also she lives at 2051 N. Clark St. The following Monday, Feb. 4, 1929, Mrs. Arvidson went to their rooms to collect her rent and found that the man in the rear

room had vacated his room and was in the front room with his friend. They said they could'nt afford to keep two rooms which she agreed to for $9.00 a week and they paid her the $9.00. The following day, Monday, Feb. 11th, 1929, she had'nt been over there and gthen they were going out about 6 p.m. they gave $9.00 to Mr. Hardway, a roomer, to give to Mrs. Arvidson, when she came over. They told her they worked nights, as Taxi Chaffeurs but she doesn't know what kind of taxis they drive. She said she was taken to the Detective Bureau by some police officers Friday afternoon, Feb. 15, 1929 to view some pictures but that she did'nt see any pictures of her roomers there. She described those men as follows:

#1, 30-35, 5-8, 150, slim build, fair complexion, brown hair, wore shell rim glasses, pearl gray fedora hat, dark overcoat.

#2, 28-30, 5-10, 155 lbs., slim build, light complexion, blond hair, thin long face, tan soft hat, gray or brown overcoat.

2. We interviewed Mrs. Alvin Pfeiffer, 2139 N. Clark St. a roomer on the second floor at above. She said she saw the man described as #1, Thursday, Feb. 14, 1929 around noon. He spoke to her and said, "Isn't it terrible, this murder across the street". He had a newspaper in his hand and went out, that is the last she saw of him. Mr. Hardway, another roomer at 2139 N. Clark St. said he thought he heard them in their room Friday morning, Feb. 15, but didn't see them and was not sure. Mrs. Arvidson said that when the newspapers are quoting her as identify pictures of her roomers, they're wrong.

(SIGNED) Devane and Connelly.

FINAL REPORT: March 26th, 1929

Death: Peter Gusenberg, 434 Roscoe St. 40 years, American, no occupation
Frank Gusenberg, 2139 Lincoln Park, west, 36 years, American, no occupation, married.
John May, 1249 W. Madison St. 35 years, American, mechanic, married
Adam Heyer, 2024 Farragut St. 40 years, American, accountant, married
Albert Weinshenk, 6320 Kenmore Av. 26 years, American, cleaner and dyer, married.
Albert Kachellek, alias James Clark, 40 years, German, no occupation, married. 6036 Gunnison.
Reinhardt Schwimmer, 2100 Lincoln Park, west, 29 years, American, optometrist, single.

Time of Death: Frank Gusenberg, 1:30 p.m. Febr. 14, 1929
All others at 10:40 a.m. February 14, 1929.

Place of Death: Frank Gusenberg at Alexian Brothers Hospital
All others at 2122 N. Clark St.

Cause of Death: Numerous Bullet Wounds.

Witnesses: Clair McAllister, 2124 N. Clark St.
Mrs. Max Landesman, 2124 N. Clark St.
Mrs. Lucy Powell, 1249 W. Madison St.
Phillip May, 1247 W. Madison St.
Josephine Morin, 2125 N. Clark St.
James Wilcox, 614 Vedder St.
Sam Schneider, 2124 N. Clark St.
Elmer Lewis, 311 S. Turner Av.

HISTORY OF CASE: At 10:45 a.m. February 14, 1929 Mrs. Landesman, 2124 N. Clark St. called the station and said there was a shooting in the garage next door at 2122 N. Clark St. Sergeant Thos. J. Loftus, Officers Geo. Love and Thos. Christy of the Auto Detail and Sergeant James Quirk, Squad 31-B, responded and entered the S.M.C. Cartage Co. garage at 2122 N. Clark St. and about half way back in the garage on the north side against the wall they found six men lying dead, shot to death with machine gun bullets. They were on a line with the wall. Peter Gusenberg was the farthest west. He was seated in a chair and hanging over the back. Next to him, lying on the floor, was Albert Weinshenk. They were fully clothed with overcoats and hats. The next on the floor was Adam Heyer, who was the owner of the garage and he was also fully clothed to hat and overcoat. Next to him was John May, 1249 W. Madison St. He was dressed in coveralls. He was a mechanic in the garage. Next to him was Reinhardt Schwimmer, who was fully dressed to overcoat and hat, and next to him was James Clark, who was dressed in a suit but no overcoat. About fifteen feet away, crawling towards the front door, was Frank Gusenberg, who said to Sergt. Loftus, "Please take me to a hospital." On the floor near him was a .38 cal. Revolver, fully loaded, which later was identified as belonging to Frank Gusenberg and on the floor about them was about was 85 empty .45 cal. Machine gun shells, and two empty shot-gun shells 12 guage, also a number of spent slugs from these cartridges, some of which had been fired thru the bodies and hit the wall. Commissioner Russell, Deputy Commissioner Wolfe, Deputy Commissioner Egan, Lieut. Hoffman and Squad, Lieut. Cusack and Squad responded. Fingerprint Department men were there and took several photos and fingerprints. Coroner Bundeson came on the scene and assumed charge of the bodies after they were searched by Lieut. Otto Erlanson and Sergeant Carney, Detective Bureau, the bodies were removed to Braithwaite's Morgue, 2129 Lincoln Av. An inquest was held on February 15th, 1929 at the Hudson Avenue Police Station and has been continued without date.

INVESTIGATION: Sergeant Thos. J. Loftus spoke to Frank Gusenberg before removal from the garage and asked him what had happened and Gusenberg said, "I wont tell, take me to a hospital." Sergeant Loftus then had him removed by the 37th District Patrol to Alexian Brothers Hospital, where the Sergeant again tried to get some informed but Gusenberg refused and he assigned Officer James Mikes at the bedside with Gusenberg until he died at 1.30 a.m. (sic) the same day, February 14, 1929. I personally interviewed Gusenberg before his death at the hospital and he told me that he would not tell me anything or would not tell me where he lived. Further investigation showed that this garage was rented on December 1, 1928 by T. Hill, 333 N. Michigan Av. to Adam Heyer under the name Frank Snyder, who told Mr. Hill that he was in the trucking business and that his trucks were working for the City of Chicago. In the garage at the time of the killing were six trucks and three automobiles, a full report of which is contained in report of Detectives Connelley and Devane attached. Among the papers of Adam Heyer, when they were looked over at the officer of Assistant States Attorney Stansbury, were found bills of sale for those cars. All of those trucks were empty, except one which contained an unassembled vat, which would have a capacity of about 500 gallons. It had never been used. Also in the papers of Heyer were found some records of the purchase of parts of the still which evidently was located on some farm in the country. A thorough search of this garage failed to show any liquor or beer, except four bottles of Canadian Ale which were found in the toilet and which apparently were for the personal use of the mechanic. Mrs. Jane Morin, 2125 N. Clark St., third floor, said she saw two men about 10.30 a.m. coming out of this garage. One of the men had his hands in the air and was followed by two men in a police uniform who were holding shot-guns towards him and the four of them got into a dark touring car with side curtains, which looked like a Cadillac and went south on Clark St. One of the men who had his hands in the air did the driving. She did not notice a license on the car. Mrs. Landesman, 2124 N. Clark St. heard shots and went to her front window and saw a man getting into a large touring car which was parked facing south on Clark St. and she then called the police. About 3.00 p.m. the same day, February 14th, 1929, Detectives Connelley and Devane arrested Henry Gusenberg, 5507 Bernice St. a brother of Peter and Frank Gusenberg, deceased, and Paddy King of the Plaza Hotel, brother-in-law of Frank Gusenberg, deceased. They found them in the lobby of the apartment hotel of 2130 Lincoln Park, west, where Frank Gusenberg lived and took them to the office of Asst. States Atty. Stansbury for questioning. On March 3rd, 1929 Sergeant Thos. Loftus went to 2130 Lincoln Park west and saw Arthur Bohnen, the manager of those apartments, and told Bohnen that he had heard that there was a machine gun found in the apartment of Frank Gusenberg after his wife had vacated the flat on February 23rd, 1929. Mr. Bohnen told him "Yes", that Oscar Cohrs, the janitor, when cleaning the apartment after being vacated, in the closet in the bedroom, underneath a small platform, he found a shotgun, a machine gun and two pistols, that he took them to his apartment on the tenth floor and that on the following day, March 1st, Paddy King, the brother-in-law of the deceased, came and asked for the guns and that he gave them to him. Cohrs and Bohnen were taken to the office of Commissioner Stege where they were questioned by Attorney Butler. Bohnen told him that he had the two revolvers down in his car in the street. These were turned over to Coroner Bundeson. Sergeant Thos. Loftus got in touch with Paddy King and he turned over a Thompson Machine Gun and 98 .45 cal. Bullets and an automatic shot-gun to Sergt. Loftus. King and the weapons were taken to Commissioner Stege's office and Commissioner Stege kept the machine gun and shot-gun.

ARRESTS: Lieut. Cusack of the Detective Burean arrested one Jack McGunrn (sic) and Officer Frank Hlavaty, Detective Bureau arrested one Albert Scalisi and they both have been indicted by the March Grand Jury for this crime.

The investigation of this crime has been conducted by States Attorney Stansbury and he has conferred with Commissioner Stege on his findings.

Investigated by: Captain Thomas Conlon,
Sergeant Thos. J. Loftus, Detectives Joseph Connelley
and John Devane, 36th District.

From the Files of the U.S. Treasury Department

The following letter was written by Internal Revenue agents and details how the successful case for tax evasion was made against Al Capone. The document is copied *ver batim,* complete with typing mistakes, misspellings and grammatical errors.

TREASURY DEPARTMENT

Internal Revenue Service
Intelligence Unit
Chicago, Illinois
July 8, 1931

CONFIDENTIAL
Internal Revenue Agent in Charge,
Chicago, Illinois.

In re: Alphonse Capone,
7244 Prairie Avenue,
Chicago, Illinois.

Alphonse Capone is, without a doubt, the best advertised and most talked about gangster in the United States today. Reams and reams of newsprint and magazine paper has been used up in exploiting Al. Capone as the "Big Shot" in his various activities as the boss of the so-called Cicero syndicate which carried on a very lucrative business in manufacturing and selling beer and alcohol, operating gambling houses and houses of prostitution.

Al Capone has been mentioned in connection with practically every major crime committed in Chicago within the last few years; possibly some of the stories are true, but, no doubt, a great deal of the stuff printed originated in the fertile brow of some newspaper reporter or magazine writer.

Al Capone, a punk hoodlum, came to Chicago from New York about 1920, as a protégé of John Torrio, who, at the time was a lieutenant of Jim Colisimo. The first heard of Capone was as a bouncer in a notoriously tough joint called the "Four Deuces". In the course of time, Colisimo, following the path of all good gangsters, was "bumped off", and Torrio took control. True to tradition, the guns again began to blaze, but this time the person behind the gun evidently had poor eyesight and Torrio, instead of going to the cemetery, took a vacation in the hospital. On getting out Torrio evidently thought discretion the better part of valor, and migrated to New York. This left the field clear for Al Capone, who promptly muscled in, and due to the free advertising in the newspapers became the "Big Shot", Capone, the immune, Capone, the idol of the hoodlum element, Capone, the dictator, free from arrest and prosecution by the local police, due, no doubt, to his lavish spending of money and giving bribes. Some time ago Capone was arrested on a vagrancy charge, and the states attorney had to dismiss the case for the reason that no policeman could be found in Chicago who knew Al Capone!

That Al Capone is shrewd, there is no doubt, which, together with his native Italian secretiveness, has made this case a most difficult one to handle. Al Capone never had a bank account and only on one occasion could be found where he ever endorsed a check, all of his financial transactions being made in currency. Agents were unable to find where he had ever purchased any securities, therefore, any evidence secured had to be developed through the testimony of associates or others, which, through fear of personal injury, or loyalty, was most difficult to obtain.

This examination, along with the cases of various other Chicago gangsters, was assigned to Internal Revenue agent W. C. Hodgins about two years ago. With the assistance of Special Agent N. E. Tessem and A. A. Martin, considerable work was done, such as making an analysis of the Pinkert State Bank remittance sheets and deposit slips for the years 1924 to 1928, from which lists were compiled of all clearing checks deposited or cashed showing the maker and last endorser. Bank accounts were analyzed, witnesses were interviewed, and every scrap of evidence possible was secured, on any of the gangsters, always with the object in view of eventually getting enough evidence together to successfully prosecute Al Capone.

This case cause such wide-spread interest that during May, 1930, Internal Revenue Agents H. N. Clagett, J. L. Westrich, and Special Agent Frank J. Wilson, were sent from the east to assist in bringing this case to a successful conclusion. From this time on Special Agent Frank J. Wilson took charge of the case, and an intensive campaign was prosecuted, developing further evidence already secured and following up every possible lead that might develop into anything of value. Outside help was solicited whenever possible, the United States District Attorney's Office was used when advantageous, witnesses were brought to Chicago and kept under guard, raids were made, telephone wires were tapped, hundreds of witnesses were interviewed, all with the object in view, not so much to develop a tax case but to sustain a criminal prosecution against Al Capone, thereby restoring to a degree the respect for Federal Laws that has not been in evidence among the gangster class during the past few years.

That agents have been successful is borne out by the fact that Ralph Capone was found guilty and is now under a three-year sentence in Leavenworth, Kansas. Jack Guzik was indicted, tried, found guilty, and sentenced to five years in Leavenworth, Kansas. He is also at liberty on an appeal.

Frank Nitto was indicted, pleaded guilty, and is now serving an eighteen months' sentence in Leavenworth, Kansas. Sam Guzik was indicted, pleaded guilty, and is now serving a one-year sentence in Leavenworth, Kansas. Louis Lipschultz was indicted and is waiting trial. Al Capone was indicted on various counts covering the years 1924 to 1929, inclusive, and on June 16, 1931, pleaded guilty to all counts in the indictment, and is now waiting to be sentenced.

On May 1, 1924, a gambling establishment was commenced in Cicero under the name of the Hawthorne Smoke Shop. During the years 1924, 1925, 1926, 1927, and 1928, this gambling establishment was raided from time to time and discontinued for short periods, and moved from one place of business to another in the immediate neighborhood, but was the same business and operated by the same people. The government has a book record made by one of the managing operators, Peter Penovich, during the year 1924, and covering its transactions during that year, and by a bookkeeper, L. A. Shumway, during the year 1925 and until April 26, 1926, (the death of States Attorney McSwiggan). The book record shows net profits for the year 1924 of approximately $300,000.00 for the year 1925 of approximately $117,000, and for the four months of January, February, March and April, of 1926, of $170,000.

The bookkeeper referred to will also testify that during the year 1924, Al Capone, Jack Guzik, Frank Nitto, Ralph Capone, Louis Alterie, Dion O'Bannion, Louis La Cava, and Johnny Torrio, came to this gambling establishment and the operating manager requested the bookkeeper to step out, inasmuch as these men desired to discuss some confidential matters relating to the business. The bookkeeper will also testify that Al Capone was very frequently in the place and conversed with the two operating managers of the business, and on one occasion he heard Al Capone suggest to them that certain people be employed. On one occasion, Al Capone asked him what he, the bookkeeper, would do if he were held up some time on his way to the bank with the profits from the business, and he replied that he would nothing, simply let them take the money. Al Capone answered that would be the correct thing to do. On the occasion of a raid on Derby Day, May 17, 1925, which will be mentioned more fully later, Al Capone directed this bookkeeper to get the funds which were in the safe, which consisted of a rather large amount of money, the exact amount not determinable, and remove them from the place that was being raided.

On the occasion of a raid which followed the murder of States' Attorney McSwiggan in 1926, the bookkeeper, at the direction of one of the operating managers of the business, removed some $84,000 from the safe of the gambling establishment and in company with this operating manager met Louis La Cava, Jack Guzik and Frank Nitto at the Atlantic Hotel and paid the money over to Louis La Cava. Just about two weeks prior to this payment, Al Capone and Louis La Cava had opened a joint safe deposit vault which neither could open except in the presence of the other. This safe deposit vault was visited occasionally for a short time both before and after this payment by Al Capone, and Louis La Cava.

On Derby Day, May 17, 1925, this gambling establishment was raided by a posse of deputy sheriffs under the leadership of a minister and a group of other citizens constituting a citizen's welfare organization from the western part of Chicago. Then this raid had first started, al Capone appeared on the scene, unshaved, with his clothes drawn hastily over his pajamas, and tried to secure admission. He was intercepted at the door, and then made the statement that he was the owner of the place, whereupon he was admitted. This statement was repeated before two reliable witnesses. On coming into the establishment where the raid was in progress, he turned to the minister and muttered a threat to the effect, "This is the last raid you'll ever pull on me." He went over to the till and started stuffing money into his pockets and designated a certain employee there to take charge of the other money on hand. He also said, "What are you fellows always picking on me?" He then left and sometime later came back shaved, fully dressed and in a pleasant humor. He asked the minister to step to one side and then said to him, "Can't we get together? If you'll let me alone here I'll withdraw from Stickney." (Stickney is a suburb where a house of prostitution had been operating and had been raided by the same organization.) The minister indicated to him that he would not be able to get together on that basis. While the gambling apparatus was being removed, one of the managers of the place asked the officers if they couldn't take one or two small pieces as evidence and leave the rest. The minister said that could not be done. Al Capone then spoke up, and, pointing to a rather large and valuable piece of gambling paraphernalia, said, "Don't take that one, that belongs to me".

In the year 1927 a casher's check in the amount of $2500 from the profits of the gambling establishment at that time bears the endorsement of Al Capone. (Al Capone is the second endorser on this check; the check is made payable to J. C. Dunbar, who was cashier of the establishment and whose name appears as the first endorsement).

Various employees will testify that Al Capone was at the gambling establishment on different occasions throughout the years of its operation and when there frequented the private office and private wire rooms where customers and employees were not allowed to go.

In the year 1924, the gambling profits were $350,250.95. Much conflicting testimony was given regarding the split for this year. However, in preparing the case for criminal prosecution, the Assistant United States Attorney handling the case requested internal revenue agents who were cooperating with them to investigate the statement of P. Penovich, Jr., to the effect that the distribution for the year 1924 was as follows:

Dion O'Bannion, represented by Dave Bates	18%
Frank Pope	18
John Torrio, represented by L. Alterie	18
P. Penovich, Jr.	5
Al Capone	41
	100%

These are the figures used in the indictment and are beliefed to be fairly correct.

On September 20, 1930, L. P. Mattingly filed with Mr. C. W. Herrick, Internal Revenue Agent in Charge, at the Chicago Office, a statement in behalf of Al Capone. In this exhibit he states "Taxpayer became active as a principal with three associates at about the end of the year 1925.

"The profits of the organization of which he was a member was divided as follows: One third to a group of four regular employees, one sixth each to the taxpayer and three associates."

The three associates referred to, it is believed, are Jack Guzik, Ralph Capone, and Frank Nitto. For the year 1925, one sixth of the total checks cashed and deposited by the three other members of the syndicate is charged to Al Capone. A small account in the name of Mae Capone, taxpayer's wife, was found in the West Side Trust and Savings Bank. The total deposits of $2500 is added to the taxpayer's income. In addition to this 52% of the Cicero gambling operations is charged to taxpayer as income, making a total of $257,339.55.

From the examination of testimony of P. Penovich, Jr. and F. Pope, at the request of the district attorney's office, it is believed the split for 1925-1926 was as follows:

Town officials	20%
Frank Pope	18
P. Penovich, Jr.	5
Ralph Capone	5
Al Capone	52
	100%

For the year 1926, income has been computed on a basis of one sixth of the total deposits and checks cashed by Jack Guzik, Ralph Capone and Frank Nitto, amounting to $107, 271.28; to this is added 52% of the Cicero gambling profits making a total of $105,677.00 gross income.

For the year 1927, in addition to checks cashed and deposits made by Jack Guzik, Ralph Capone, and Frank Nitto, the deposits of Sam Guzik were also considered as income of the syndicate. Large sums were transferred to Jack Guzik and it is believed he was a collector for the syndicate. One sixth of the checks cashed and deposited amounts to $205,557.04, to which is added $10,000 investment in Hawthorne Kennel Club, and a cashier's check cashed, makes a total gross income of $218,057.04. During the Guzik trial, Fred Ries, alias J. C. Dunbar, testified he purchased about $134,000 in cashier's checks which represented surplus of the gambling houses he worked for owned by the syndicate. $46,000 of these were cashed by Jack Guzik, the balance being deposited. During the year the Hawthorne Kennel Club was organized. It now appears that Al Capone had an investment of $10,000 in this corporation and it is not known how he acquired this stock, same is added to income. Likewise, a cashier's check purchased by Fred Ries, alias J. C. Dunbar, for $2500, and cashed by taxpayer, personally.

For the year 1928, income was computed on a basis of one sixth of Jack Guzik, Ralph Capone and Sam Guzik, which amounts to $147,205.59; to this is added a $10,000 Liberty Bond purchased at The First National Bank, Cicero, and turned over to the Roosevelt Finance Company in payment of a loan.

In 1928, approximately $72,000 was sent from Chicago to Al Capone, in Florida, by wire transfer at irregular intervals in amounts of approximately $2000 or thereabouts. Some of the transfers are as low as $300 and some run as high as $5000. These transfers were sent during a period of five or six months, some transfers being sent daily and sometimes with intervals of four or five weeks elapsing between transfers.

These transfers were sent from Chicago by Rocco Fischetti, (who was seen frequently with Al Capone in gambling establishments), Joe Fusco, George Howlett, Sam Guzik (brother of Jack Guzik, Capone's chief lieutenant and business manager), and Bobby Barton, Bobby Barton was the recipient of cashier's checks from the cashier of one of the gambling establishments and deposited many of these checks in Jack Guzik's bank account. He was messenger and chauffeur for Jack Guzik.

These wire transfers in a few cases were sent to Al Capone in his own name and in most cases to him under the name A. Costa, who can be identified as Al Capone by Western Union employees.

Mr. Mattingly, in his letter to Mr. Herrick, admits income of $100,000 for 1929, but inasmuch as the rough draft of this letter reads $2000 a month, income has been fixed at $104,000. A deduction of $1.00 has been allowed for all years.

That the syndicate is selling beer is certain. During the Ralph Capone trial checks were traced from Ralph Capone's bank account to Hak Brothers and John Kunz. Mr. Miles Hak and Mr. Kunz testified these checks were given in payment of beer. That they were in the alcohol business is equally certain. Many checks drawn on the account of Max Altersohn was cashed by Frank Nitto. Mr. Altersohn states that these checks were given in payment of alcohol; also a statement from another witness in Davenport, Iowa, saying L. Lipschultz from whom he purchased alcohol, told him (the witness) that he (L. Lipschultz) was working for Al Capone.

Some time ago Special Agents Malone and Sullivan were drafted into the case for the purpose of developing evidence that would connect the syndicate with several houses of prostitution located in Stickney, Illinois. Several of Jack Guzik's checks were traced to the Maple Building Corporation, in payment on the building housing a notorious joint called The Stockade. It is believed that Special Agents Sullivan and Malone were making progress in developing evidence to establish ownership of the syndicate on the Harlem Inn and the Shadow Inn, both in Stickney, Illinois, when the case broke and Al Capone pleaded guilty.

The only known assets of Al Capone is his home in Florida. Two automobiles partly paid for, personal effects, and his stock in the Hawthorne Kennel Club.

The report is made as near as possibly in accordance with the figures used in the indictments. Changes were made for the years 1925 and 1927, due to correction of figures, otherwise the figures used are the same.

This case, while it has been long drawn out and very difficult in come respects, has been brought to a successful conclusion and agents feel the results accomplished have justified the time and energy used.

Agents wish to take this opportunity to thank Mr. A. P. Madden for his fine spirit and cooperation throughout the examination, Mr. Frank Wilson for his patience and forbearance, when everything seemed to go wrong, for the consideration of his welfare and the comfort of the men working with him, for his advise and council, and his willingness to put his shoulder to the wheel whenever needed to carry the load over the hill; Mr. Nels Teessem, for his bulldog tenacity in holding on until the last scrap of evidence has been extracted; other members of the Intelligence Unit for their splendid help and cooperation when needed, and the district attorney's office and its various members for their advice and council on the law.

The moral shown in this case has been wonderful. Nobody shirked – on the contrary, everybody we think did their very best at the particular task they were assigned, all working for a common good, and this we believe is what put the case over.

W. C. Hodgins,
Internal Revenue Agent.

Jacque L. Westrich,
Internal Revenue Agent.

H. N. Clagett,
Internal Revenue Agent.